STUDY GUIDE
to accompany
NASH·JEFFREY
HOWE · FREDERICK · DAVIS · WINKLER

THE AMERICAN PEOPLE

CREATING A NATION AND A SOCIETY

Second Edition

VOLUME ONE · Beginnings to 1877

JULIE ROY JEFFREY
Goucher College

PETER J. FREDERICK
Wabash College

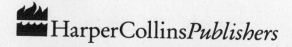
HarperCollinsPublishers

Study Guide to accompany Nash/Jeffrey et al. THE AMERICAN PEOPLE Vol. 1 to 1877, 2

Copyright © 1990 by HarperCollins*Publishers*, Inc.

ISBN: 0-06-044738-9

90 91 92 93 94 9 8 7 6 5 4 3 2

CONTENTS

"A people without history is like
wind upon the buffalo grass."
                        --Lakota Sioux

Acknowledgements

Our ideas about teaching and learning have several sources, but none so important as those interactions and friendships with our students over the past 25 years at Rice University and California State University at Hayward, but especially at Goucher College and Wabash College. In particular, we are grateful for the invaluable help of three student assistants, Jane Golberg, George T. Patton, and Zhen-ming Tan, in preparing these study guides (and much in the textbook itself). George worked with us as a colleague one summer on both the guides and the RTPs, and Tan was indispensable in helping us prepare this second edition.

Tan, Patsy Teague, an exceptional typist and problem-solver, and the Wabash College Computer Center, David Maharry, Jasmine Robinson, and Alice Moore in particular, deserve credit as the effective printers of these volumes. To them our heartfelt thanks.

"The value of History is, indeed, not scientific but moral:
by liberalizing the mind, by deepening the sympathies, by
fortifying the will, it enables us to control, not society,
but ourselves... and to meet the future."
                        --Carl L. Becker

INTRODUCTION
How to Pass Your History Course by Rediscovering the Past

In one of Garry Trudeau's "Doonesbury" cartoons, Mike and Zonker are strolling through the woods as Zonker reminisces about their college days. Among other things, he says, they went on study dates in the boat house, held midnight sledding parties, parked the dean's Volvo inside the chapel, got busted at a rock concert, and ran naked through a meeting of the board of trustees. After listening to Zonker's recollections of those "bright college years," Mike reminds him that "we never did any of those things." Zonker agrees, saying, "I know, but one day we'll think we did." "Isn't it a little early to start embellishing?" Mike asks. Zonker coolly responds, "You gotta grab the past while you can!"

We introduce the Study Guide to The American People: Creating a Nation and a Society with this cartoon for two reasons. First, we are aware that the conflicting demands and pressures of college life often lead students to pranks, pizza parlors, parties, and paper deadline panics--the kinds of events that stimulated Zonker's imagination. Exaggerated and embellished as his fantasies were, they suggest the range of experiences we know students go through, or think about, during their college years. We certainly did. Our current fantasy is that you might add the study of American history to the positive college experiences that you will remember in later years--not made up, like Zonker's, but for real!
We have prepared this Study Guide, therefore, to smooth your way through the American history textbook, not as a substitute for it but as a supplement--a guide to reading The American People for maximum understanding, appreciation, enjoyment and, yes, success on examinations. To be sure, you have many long hours of reading, reflection, and study ahead of you. Studying history is not easy. But it can be pleasurable as well as profitable, and we sincerely hope that you will find your study of American history almost as enjoyable--and certainly as educational--as the diversions that Zonker imagined as a college student.

1

We also introduce this guide with Trudeau's cartoon because the last lines say something significant not only about students but also about historians. Although professionally committed to telling the truth about the past, which for the most part they succeed in doing, historians tend sometimes, like Zonker, to "embellish." Like any good storytellers, historians enjoy building an exciting drama by the addition of juicy adjectives and heightened tension. Occasionally they even get a date or name wrong. At one level this is inexcusable, and historians try to check and doublecheck their facts so as never to make errors. But they are only human, and both the authors of your textbook and your history professor may sometimes embellish or make mistakes. So will you, but your errors will be marked wrong. The ultimate responsibility for "getting the history right," therefore, is yours.

Historians also embellish when they interpret the past, not by telling inflated stories or committing factual errors but simply by showing their human point of view, which is the result of their particular time, place, circumstances, and personal backgrounds. Such factors influence the selection and interpretation of past events. Interpretation is unavoidable, and students should beware of a book or person that claims to be "the truth" rather than one interpretation of the truth.

All works of history, even textbooks, present a point of view reflecting the values, assumptions, and interests of the author. Interpretation differs from a biased presentation in that the latter willfully distorts truth while the former deepens understanding by the process of explaining how and why things happened in the past. This makes the writing (and teaching) of history more than a listing of names, dates, and other facts. The act of interpretation is a humble one, and you should be looking for the interpretive point of view of the authors of your textbook as you read. The Preface is a good place to start.

The history presented in The American People is enriched by an interpretive framework. It tells the story of the many ways in which the diverse people coming to this country--whether on foot across the Bering Straits, on rafts across the Rio Grande, or on the Mayflower, slave ships, or immigrant steamers--created a cultural mosaic of many societies, and one nation. These individual stories are the history, or "story," of "the American people." Our major goal is to help you both learn and enjoy this story. In the 1990s, as we continue to seek to know who we are by knowing where we came from, we realize that, like Michael Doonesbury, "you gotta grab the past while you can."

IMPORTANT ASSUMPTIONS TO BE AWARE OF

Toward that end, we have prepared this Study Guide. Your teacher has a similar one. We believe that you should know some of our most important assumptions as we prepared the textbook and these guides. They are as follows:

1. The authors have tried to write a textbook that is not just a series of historical names, dates, places, and other facts--"one damned thing after another," as someone once described history. Rather, we show history as the story of the daily lives of both ordinary and famous Americans in the past. We have sought to take you inside these lives, to experience the fears, frustrations, and aspirations of the American people.

2. We want you not only to reexperience these lives but also to be confident that you remember what you have studied. When learning history is real in terms of your own experiences, as well as fun, you tend to do better on tests.

3. We believe that the textbook and guides are only as good as they are teachable and learnable. We have designed both the text and these guides to be immediately usable, if an instructor desires, for a variety of classroom learning activities and assignments that enrich student learning and the appreciation of American history.

4. We believe that students become historians themselves the minute they open their textbooks and begin to read them. When you consulted your list of classes and other sources in order to discover what history course you signed up for and at what time and in what room it met, you were already acting as a historian, recovering a small piece of your own past in order to understand the present. We have designed a special feature in every chapter, called "Recovering the Past," to show the variety of ways in which <u>all</u> historians, including yourselves, work to construct the past.

5. We believe that students--all people, in fact--learn best when they begin with a personally compelling human experience, their own or someone else's. This human story suggests further stories, or facts, and some overarching themes and concepts. These are in turn analyzed, interpreted, compared to other facts,

3

applied to other settings, and evaluated. Finally, there must be an opportunity to express what one has learned and to receive feedback on how well. We have structured the textbook and this guide according to this basic pattern of human learning.

HOW TO UNDERSTAND A CHAPTER

Take Chapter 1, for example, which begins with the tragic story of Opechancanough, a Powhatan tribesman whose entire life of nearly 90 years was consumed by a struggle against the land hunger and alien values brought by Spanish and English newcomers to his ancestral lands in present-day Virginia near the Chesapeake Bay. After surviving germs brought by the Spanish and fighting many battles against English settlers near Jamestown, Opechancanough was captured and executed.

The brief anecdote about Opechancanough introduces most of the overarching themes and major concepts of Chapter 1: the intermingling in the North American wilderness of three worlds--red, white, and black--each with different life styles, cultural values, and aspirations. The result of this contact was terrible for the Native Americans, whether living in Spanish-controlled Central and South America or near English settlements in North America. Opechancanough's death at the hands of an English jailer in 1646 foreshadowed the destruction of Native Americans and their way of life by Europeans in coming centuries. Furthermore, the Spanish and English, though both white Europeans, were locked in a combat with each other that had serious effects on the development of the Americas. In each chapter of the textbook, an anecdote of an ordinary person's life will, like the one about Opechancanough, suggest the crucial themes of the chapter. Therefore, it is important to pay special attention to the elements of each story to see how it reveals the chapter's major concepts.

The bedrock of history, as many history students have found out to their despair, is composed of facts. Broad historical themes are the handles, or pegs, upon which to hang the many particular facts that make up the past. These facts must be mastered--often by memorization--in order to provide life and substance to the larger themes. In Chapter 1, for example, there are a number of names, dates, places, and terms. Once you are familiar with major concepts like the collision of three cultures and the disastrous outcome for Native Americans, these facts can be placed in some category, or hung on some peg, and are therefore easier to remember.

Think, for example, of how you would remember the following facts: names such as Cortes, Elizabeth I, and Incas; dates such as "pre-Columbian," 1492, and 1607; places such as Peru, Venice, and Roanoke Island; and terms such as matrilineal, the Reformation, and "the great dying."

Once the facts are mastered within the context of the major themes, you are able to work with, or use, both facts and concepts in a more sophisticated way than just repeating or listing them. You could, for example, contrast the three worlds according to their differing values and beliefs about nature, religion, family, and political and economic goals. Or you could analyze the reasons for the conflict between Spain and England. Or you could apply or transfer your knowledge to similar situations, like the intermingling and conflicts today, perhaps even in your own community, among ethnic and racial groups with differing sets of values. Or you might evaluate how people thought and felt about the effects of the clash of cultures in both the seventeenth and twentieth centuries. Being able to form judgments like these is the highest level of learning and depends upon a prior understanding of specific facts and thematic concepts.

Finally, to check how well you have learned the material of a chapter, it is good to be tested--on both the specific facts and the larger themes of that chapter. This feedback is necessary both to confirm your confidence in how much has been learned and to identify areas that need further study.

To summarize, most people learn best by moving through the following sequence:

1. Engagement in a human story
2. An overview of major themes and concepts
3. Mastery of specific facts that support or illustrate those themes
4. Analysis, synthesis, comparison, application, and evaluation of the themes
5. An opportunity to demonstrate knowledge practicing these steps on tests and other assignments

Each chapter in The American People can be understood better by studying it in terms of this basic learning pattern.

HOW TO USE THE STUDY GUIDE WITH THE TEXT

The Study Guide also follows this pattern. Students who work back and forth from the chapter in The American People to the chapter in the guide will continually be reinforcing and strengthening their mastery and enjoyment of American history. With a little experimenting, students will find that it is sometimes better to read the textbook chapter before looking at the guide and sometimes better to read the guide before the textbook.

Each chapter contains the following sections:

(1) Chapter Outline (with opening anecdote)

It is helpful to look through the outline before reading a chapter in order to see at a glance both the major topics to be covered and the chapter's organization. The short summary of the human story or anecdote that begins each chapter should point toward these topics and suggest the structure.

(2) Significant Themes And Highlights

Three or four statements will provide an overview summary of the main themes, concepts, threads, major ideas, and special features of each chapter. To consult this section before reading the chapter may be the most helpful thing you can do in order to have some handles or pegs to help you understand and place the many particular facts encountered in the chapter. Keeping these major concepts in mind as you read will prevent you from getting lost in a sea of facts. Specific facts are valuable to a historian only as illustrations of some larger theme. If you have a strong sense of the themes you will more easily remember the appropriate illustrative factual examples when taking examinations.

(3) Learning Goals Of The Chapter

The list of the goals, or objectives, of each chapter is a way of providing a self-check on how well you are mastering the material. After completing a chapter, try answering each item. If you can, you are ready to move on. If you cannot, you know which topics to review in the chapter. When you are preparing for examinations, reread the sections on learning goals for the appropriate chapters.

The first five to six learning goals indicate the "basic knowledge" you should be familiar with--the essential facts every history student has to know before doing anything else. Such knowledge is usually tested with short-answer exam questions: multiple-choice, true-or-false, identification, fill-in-the-blanks, and similar formats. You also need to know these facts in order to handle more difficult kinds of questions. The second part of the learning goals section includes three goals intended to give you "Practice in Historical Thinking Skills," higher-order learning tasks such as analyzing, comparing and contrasting, applying, assessing, and evaluating historical phenomena. This is what we mean by interpretation. These intellectual skills are usually tested by essay questions and paper assignments. You can prepare for these by writing short practice essays on these three learning goals.

(4) Important Dates And Names To Know

Nothing drives history students crazier than having to memorize dates. Yet chronology--the order and sequence of past events--is essential to understanding history. What is most important for students to remember is not that they must memorize every exact date but rather that they should form a general idea of the sequence in which events happened. Remembering key dates is not as mysterious as students often think: it is usually just a matter of common sense. One could, for example, remember that the Declaration of Independence was signed in 1776 and the Constitution in 1787, but what is really important is to get them in the right order. Imagine how silly it would be to reverse them. It is common sense that the bonds of one government had to be dissolved before a new one could be created. The chronologies of important dates will usually include important names to remember as well. Names that are not associated with a particular date but are nevertheless significant are listed at the end of the chronology.

(5) Glossary Of Important Terms

Although history is not nearly as filled with jargon and special vocabularies as other disciplines, various unfamiliar terms inevitably turn up in every chapter. These are listed and briefly identified in this section. Remember that your teachers may also have favorite terms that they want you to learn, so it is a good idea to add them to these lists.

(6) Enrichment Ideas

We think this is the most important section in the guides. In this part is a list of activities and assignments designed to aid and enhance learning of the important themes and concepts in each chapter. Some are activities you can follow and do on your own. A longer list, not included in the Student Guide, contains assignments and classroom activities your instructor may want to use. The variety of suggested approaches to enrich learning--both in the class-room and out--is extensive, but they always begin with further ways of using the "Recovering the Past" feature. This section, found in each chapter, is intended to introduce students of history to the many sources and ways in which historians find out what happened in the past.

A century ago, most historians would probably have said that they recovered the past by reading old manuscripts, primarily government and other institutional documents housed in official archives, and by consulting the letters, papers, and manuscripts of former presidents, senators, generals, and other leaders. But in recent years, as historians have broadened their interest from political and military history (unkindly called "drum and trumpets" history), to include the social history of ordinary people, they have also widened the kinds of sources they find useful in recovering the past. To written government documents and archival manuscripts his-torians have added private diaries, popular songs, paintings, cartoons, census returns, tax and inventory lists, films and photographs, material objects, oral history, and many other means of recovering the past.

The "RTPs", as the authors affectionately call them, are intended not only to enrich your learning of American history but also to show you how you can become your own historian. For the most part, each means of recovering the past is appropriate to the content of the chapter in which it is found. Thus the work of archaeologists and the contributions archaeology makes to understanding earlier civilizations are discussed in Chapter 1; folktales in the chapter on slavery; and films, oral history, and television in the twentieth-century chapters. Additional ways of recovering the past, such as popular Hollywood feature films and trips to historical areas, are mentioned in the appropriate Enrichment sections in this Study Guide.

(7) Sample Test And Examination Questions

Many students will find this section most useful in preparing for examinations, not because their teachers will necessarily select test questions from those included (though they might) but because students can check for themselves how well they have learned the material in a chapter. Note that the sample questions begin with short-answer types (multiple choice, matching, etc.) to test basic knowledge (how well you remember the material), whereas the later questions are essays and interpretive questions that test historical thinking skills (how well you can compare and contrast, analyze, interpret, apply, and evaluate the main ideas of the chapter). In these higher-order questions, you gain practice in learning how to think like historians, doing the kind of basic detective groundwork interpreting evidence from various sources and writing analytic essays.

The test questions for some chapters in this guide end with a map question, which is a lower-order but fundamentally important content knowledge skill (knowing where places are). Other chapters end with a quotation, chart, or other verbal or quantitative illustration, which we ask you to identify and interpret--who, what, where, when, and why significant. This is a more sophisticated exercise in the detection and interpretation of a historical source.

HOW TO UNDERLINE A CHAPTER

One of the first problems students face when they begin reading a textbook is how much to underline or highlight. A consideration of the purpose of underlining may help guide you through a chapter. The major goal, of course, is to aid memory and comprehension by highlighting the main themes, selecting important examples for each major idea. This helps not only to understand the chapter but also to review for examinations. Too little underlining means that you may end up rereading the entire chapter the night before a test. Too much, in which no discrimination has taken place, may also mean having to reread everything. It is, of course, important to note the topic sentences for each paragraph. In addition, pay particular attention to the one or two paragraphs that make the transition from the opening anecdote to the main body of the chapter. These state the major themes and often even the organization of the chapter.

The box shows an example of how we would underline the transition paragraph and a short section from Chapter 1.

Over a long lifetime, Opechancanough painfully experienced the meeting of people from three continents. His land was one of many that would be penetrated by Europeans over the next three centuries, as Christian civilization girdled the globe. On the Chespeake Bay, this clash of cultures formed the opening chapter of what we know as American history. That history, in turn, was one scene in a much broader drama of European colonization and exploitation of many indigenous cultures thousands of miles from the Old World. The nature of this violent intermingling of Europeans, Africans, and Na- ① ② ③ tive Americans is an essential part of early American history. But to understand how the destinies of red, white, and black people ③ ① ② became intertwined in Opechancanough's land, we must look at the precontact history and cultural foundations of life in the homelands of each of them.

9

Contrasting World Views

Colonizing Europeans called themselves "civilized" and typically described the people they met in the Americas as "savage," "heathen," or "barbarian." But the gulf separating people in Europe and North America was not defined so much by how the two cultures extracted a food supply from the land, housed themselves, or organized family life as by how they viewed their relationship to the environment and defined social relations in their communities. In these areas, a wide difference in values existed. This created the potential for a dangerous conflict once the Atlantic Ocean that had separated two ancient civilizations had been transformed from a barrier to a bridge by a technological and scientific leap forward by western Europeans in the fifteenth century.

In the view of Europeans the natural world was a resource designed for man's use. "Subdue the earth," read the first book of the Old Testament, "and have dominion over every living thing that moves on the earth." God ruled the cosmos, bringing floods, droughts, and earthquakes, but humans could reshape their physical surroundings into a productive and secure world. Man's relationship to the natural environment was a secular matter, even if God, in the sacred sphere, sometimes intervened.

Native Americans, in contrast, were "a people that are contented with Nature as they find her," as one colonist phrased it. In their ethos, every part of the natural environment was sacred. Rocks, trees, and animals all possessed spiritual power, and all were linked to form a sacred whole. To injure the environment, by overfishing or abusing it in any way, was to offend the spiritual power present throughout nature and hence to risk spiritual retaliation. In the villages of Europe, peasant people had similarly believed in spirits residing in trees and rocks, but such "superstition" was fading.

Regarding the soil as a resource to be exploited for man's benefit, Europeans believed that land should be privately possessed. Individual ownership of property became a fundamental concept, and an extensive institutional apparatus grew up to support it. Fences symbolized private property, inheritance became the mechanism for transmitting land from one generation to another within the same family, and courts gained the power to settle property disputes. Property was the basis not only of sustenance but also of independence, material wealth, political status, and personal identity. The social structure directly mirrored patterns of land ownership, with a land-wealthy elite at the apex of the social pyramid and a mass of propertyless individuals forming the broad base.

Native Americans also had concepts of property, and tribes recognized territorial boundaries. But they believed that land was invested with sacred qualities and should be held in common. As one German missionary to the Delaware Indians explained their view in the eighteenth century, the Creator "made the Earth and all that it contains for the common good of mankind. Whatever liveth on the land, whatsoever groweth out of the earth, and all that is in the rivers and waters . . . was given jointly to all and everyone is entitled to his share."

Communal ownership sharply limited social stratification in most tribal communities. Accustomed to wide disparities of wealth, Europeans often found this remarkable. Observing the Iroquois of the eastern woodlands in 1657, a French Jesuit noted with surprise that they had no almshouses because "their kindness, humanity and courtesy not only makes them liberal with what they have, but causes them to possess hardly anything except in common. A whole village must be without corn, before any individual can be obliged to endure privation." Not all Europeans were acquisitive, competitive individuals. The majority were peasants scratching a subsistence living from the soil, living in kin-centered villages with little contact with the outside world, and exchanging goods and labor through barter. But in Europe's urban centers a wealth-conscious, striving individual who celebrated wider choices and greater opportunities to enhance personal status was coming to the fore. In contrast, Native American traditions stressed the group rather than the individual. Holding land and other resources in common, Indian societies were usually more egalitarian and their members more concerned with personal valor than personal wealth.

Exceptions to this cultural system occurred in the highly developed and populous Aztec and Inca empires and, in North America, among a few tribes such as the Natchez. But on the eastern and western coasts of the continent and in the Southwest—the regions of contact in the sixteenth and seventeenth centuries—the European newcomers encountered a people whose cultural values differed strikingly from theirs.

European colonizers in North America also found disturbing the matrilineal organization of many tribal societies. Contrary to European practice, family membership among the Iroquois, for example, was determined through the female line.

PART ONE

A COLONIZING PEOPLE
1492-1776

1

Three Worlds Meet

(1) CHAPTER OUTLINE

For his entire life of 90 years in the Chesapeake Bay region, the Powhatan tribesman Opechancanough struggled to defend his land and way of life against the intrusions of the Spanish and English (and even Africans), thus showing how the lives of red, white, and black people were intertwined in North America.

The People of America Before Columbus

    Hunters and Farmers
    Native Americans in 1600
    Contrasting World Views

Africa on the Eve of Contact

    The Kingdoms of Africa
    The African Ethos

Europe in the Age of Exploration

    The Rise of Europe
    The New Monarchies and the Expansionist Impulse
    Reaching the Americas
    Religious Conflict During the Reformation

The Iberian Conquest of America

The Spanish Onslaught
The Great Dying
Silver, Sugar, and Their Consequences
Spain's Northern Frontier

England Goes West

England Challenges Spain
The Westward Fever
Anticipating North America

Conclusion: Converging Worlds

(2) SIGNIFICANT THEMES AND HIGHLIGHTS

1. The clash of three cultures from three continents
    --North America, Europe, and Africa--forms the
    opening chapter of American history and is therefore
    the opening chapter of the textbook. With
    Opechancanough's life story we see the collision and
    intermingling of three worlds, red, white, and black.
    The converging of cultural values and aspirations,
    often accompanied by violence and disease, disrupted
    and nearly destroyed the red world, enslaved the
    victims from the black world, and furthered the
    expansion and development of the white world.

2. A secondary clash within the European white world,
    that between Catholic Spain and Protestant England,
    explains the different development of Spanish Central
    and South America and English North America.

3. By taking readers inside the cultural beliefs and
    experiences of Native Americans and Africans, as well
    as Europeans, this chapter serves to counteract the
    traditional ethnocentric view that sees all
    developments through the eyes of Europeans. An
    example of this is the oft-repeated phrase, "Columbus
    discovered America," implying that there was no life
    or culture in the Americas until a European found it
    in 1492.

(3) LEARNING GOALS

Familiarity with Basic Knowledge

After reading this chapter, you should be able to:

1. Locate and briefly describe the Native American Mound Builders of the Ohio and Mississippi river valleys, the Pueblo dwellers of the Southwest, and the woodland Indians of the East Coast.

2. Describe Native American attitudes toward and beliefs about the natural world, wealth, community, family, and men and women.

3. Name and locate three West African kingdoms between the fifth and fourteenth centuries and describe West African beliefs about family, religion, and social organization.

4. Explain the political, economic, religious, and technological changes in early modern Europe that led to the exploration and eventual settlement of North America.

5. Locate on a map the names and routes of the most significant Iberian, English, French, and Dutch explorers and conquerors in the fifteenth and sixteenth centuries.

6. Describe the impact of the European conquest of the Americas on the Native American Indian population.

Practice in Historical Thinking Skills

After reading this chapter, you should be able to:

1. Compare and contrast the values and life styles of the three worlds--red, white, and black--that met in the Americas early in the sixteenth century.

2. Evaluate the outcomes of that collision for each world. What do you think and feel about these outcomes?

3. Compare and contrast the cultures of Spain and England, and their motivations for settling the Americas.

(4) IMPORTANT DATES AND NAMES TO KNOW

Pre-Columbian epochs:

12,000 B.C.	Beringian epoch ends
500 B.C.	Archaic era ends
500 B.C.-A.D. 1500	Post-Archaic era in North America Kingdoms of Ghana, Mali, Songhay and Benin in Africa
1420s	Portuguese sailors explore west coast of Africa
1492	Christopher Columbus lands on Caribbean islands Spanish expel Moors (Moslems)
1494	Treaty of Tordesillas
1497-1585	French and British explore northern part of the Americas
1498	Vasco da Gama reaches India after sailing around Africa
1513	Portuguese explorers reach China
1521	Cortés captures Mexico City, conquering the Aztecs
1533	Pizarro captures Cuzco, conquering the Incas
1515-1565	Spanish explore Florida and southern part of North America
1540-1542	Coronado explores the Southwest
1520s	Luther attacks Catholicism
1530s	Calvin calls for religious reform
1558	Elizabeth I crowned queen of England
1585	Roanoke Island settlement
1588	English defeat the Spanish Armada

| 1603 | James I succeeds Elizabeth I |
| 1607 | English begin settlement at Jamestown, Virginia |

Other Names to Know

Prince Henry the Navigator	Ponce de Leon
Hernando de Soto	John Cabot
Jacques Cartier	Verrazano
Richard Hakluyt	Cahokia

(5) GLOSSARY OF IMPORTANT TERMS

<u>Pre-Columbian era:</u> the period of history before Columbus in which Native American Indian cultures lived in the Americas undiscovered--and unaffected--by Europeans

<u>matrilineal</u>: tracing descent and property and political rights through the mother

<u>Renaissance</u>: period of cultural rebirth in Europe (fifteenth-sixteenth centuries)

<u>Protestant Reformation:</u> period in Europe in the sixteenth century of protest against the Roman Catholic church and the creation of new (Protestant) religious institutions

<u>Muslim:</u> a person believing in the religion of Islam, which began in the seventh century and spread throughout the Middle East and northern Africa and eventually to Asia and Europe in succeeding centuries (Muslims, or Moslems, were sometimes called Moors by Europeans)

(6) ENRICHMENT IDEAS

1. Find out which Native American tribes and nations lived in your part of the country and whether there are any archaeological working sites or remains, like Cahokia, to visit. Also visit any museums or historical parks that feature local Indian history.

2. Pretend that you are an archaeologist or anthropologist who wants to understand and reconstruct in your region as much of the original Indian culture and typical daily life as possible

15

from relics and other remains. Present your findings
to others in various forms: oral report, written
paper, table display showing artifacts and a model of
Indian life, or artistic drawings or skits
illustrating Indian culture.

3. Pretend that you are an archaeologist or
anthropologist from some distant future who wants to
understand and reconstruct as much as possible of
present-day culture and daily life in your community.
Imagine the absolute destruction of all written
records and the near-destruction and burying under
dirt and debris of material objects and structures.
As you dig up the remains or observe unusual
topological and other features (like dammed-up
streams, terraced and flattened hills, or roadway
patterns), how much of the original daily life and
culture do you think you could reconstruct?

4. Imagine yourself as a Martian, who has never seen
Earthlings, arriving to explore and settle the planet
Earth. From the behavior of human beings what kind of
conclusions might you draw about their cultural
patterns and values? What images do you have about
groups different from your own? Think about both
positive and negative images.

5. Look over the opening anecdote. Imagine yourself as
Opechancanough going through the various epochs of
his life. Write a speech or memoir on what he might
have thought about the values and cultural norms of
white people in the different seasons of his life.

(7) SAMPLE TEST AND EXAMINATION QUESTIONS

Multiple choice: Choose the best answer.

1. The "New World" was first entered by people from the
   "Old World"
   a. about 12,000 to 28,000 years ago
   b. about 5,000 to 10,000 years ago
   c. in about A.D 1000
   d. in 1492

2. The greatest loss of life for Native Americans during
   the sixteenth and seventeenth centuries was caused
   by:
   a. intertribal warfare
   b. intermarriage with Europeans

16

    c. conversion to European religions
    d. infectious bacteria brought by Europeans

3. Cahokia was the center of
    a. "Hopewell" culture
    b. "Mississippi" culture
    c. "Pueblo" culture
    d. "Iroquois" culture

4. According to Native Americans before the European
    invasion
    a. the natural world was a resource for man's use
    b. every part of the natural environment was sacred
    c. the belief that spirits resided in nature was
        fading
    d. land was the basis of status and identity

5. From the fifth to the fourteenth centuries, West
    Africa
    a. was a savage land of nomadic hunters
    b. was colonized and exploited by various European
        nations
    c. was engaged in perpetual warfare with Muslims
        from the Middle East
    d. featured the development of a series of kingdoms
        with relatively advanced cultures and complex
        political structures

6. In the fifteenth century, West African societies
    a. developed an extensive industrial system based
        on slaves captured in tribal wars
    b. had the most brutal system of slavery in the
        civilized world
    c. respected the privileges of education and
        marriage and the protection of the law for slaves
    d. provided legal protection and rights only for
        slave children

7. By the fifteenth and sixteenth centuries a new
    political entity, _____, had arisen in Europe.
    a. dictatorships
    b. democracies
    c. feudal states
    d. nation-states

8. All of the following changes in fifteenth-century
    Europe led to an expansionist impulse except
    a. the rise of new monarchies
    b. the rise of Calvinism
    c. technological improvements
    d. trade rivalry with the Muslims

17

9. According to Martin Luther,
   a. only a chosen few deserved salvation
   b. only non-Catholics could ever be saved
   c. salvation came through faith in God's grace
   d. salvation was earned through good works

   B (handwritten)

10. The Treaty of Tordesillas divided settlement of the Americas between
    a. Spain and Portugal
    b. Spain and England
    c. Spain and France
    d. France and England

    B (handwritten)

11. What percentage of the inhabitants of the Aztec empire died of diseases brought by the Spanish?
    a. 20 percent
    b. 50 percent
    c. 75 percent
    d. 90 percent

12. Which of the following best describes England's motivations for moving westward to North America?
    a. the quest for new fisheries
    b. the quest for gold and silver
    c. religious and trading rivalry with Spain
    d. the desire to Christianize heathen Indians

    B (handwritten)

13. Which of the following pairs is not correct?
    a. Pizarro - Incas
    b. Cortés - Aztecs
    c. de Soto - New Mexico and Arizona
    d. Ponce de León - Florida

    B (handwritten)

14. Early European images of the "New World"
    a. described an earthly paradise full of riches
    b. depicted friendly native inhabitants
    c. pictured backward, hostile savages
    d. described all of the above

    A (handwritten)

Essays

1. Compare and contrast Native American and European beliefs and practices about the natural world, property and wealth, and community and family life.

2. Analyze English motivations for exploring and eventually settling the New World.

3. Evaluate the converging of three worlds--red, black, and white--in the Americas. What was gained and what was lost by each of the three?

4. "Neither the Spanish nor the English respected Indian culture and society; this lack of respect enabled them to destroy Native American life with few regrets." Write an essay supporting this statement, selecting appropriate evidence.

2

Colonizing a Continent

(1) CHAPTER OUTLINE

Captain John Mason leaves the Massachusetts Bay Colony with other Puritans in search of better lands. They establish the new community of Windsor on the Connecticut River. Shortly afterward, Mason leads hundreds of the settlers in an attack on the Pequot Indians, massacring them.

The Chesapeake Tobacco Coast

    Jamestown
    Sot Weed and Indentured Servants
    Expansion and Indian War
    Proprietary Maryland
    Daily Life on the Chesapeake

Massachusetts and Its Offspring

    Puritanism in England
    Puritan Predecessors in New England
    Errand into the Wilderness
    An Elusive Utopia
    New Englanders and Indians
    The Web of Village Life

From the St. Lawrence to the Hudson

> England Challenges the Mighty Dutch
> Proprietary Carolina: A Restoration Reward
> The Indian Debacle
> Early Carolina Society

The Quakers' Peaceable Kingdom

> The Early Friends
> Early Quaker Designs
> Pacifism in a Militant World:
> Quakers and Indians
> Building the Peaceable Kingdom
> The Limits of Perfectionism

Conclusion: The Achievement of New Societies

(2) SIGNIFICANT THEMES AND HIGHLIGHTS

1. A theme running throughout the chapter, illustrated by the Pequot massacre, is the confrontation in North America between two cultures: the English colonists (in various kinds of settlements) and the Native American Indians. The two cultures collided as the colonists sought to realize the goals that had lured them to the New World and the Indians sought to defend their tribal homelands.

2. A second theme focuses on tensions growing out of the religious and economic motivations behind settlement. Many English colonists came to America to create religious utopias, a New World Zion. Others, even in the same settlement, came for economic opportunity, gold, and land. Regardless of motive, the colonists experienced limits to their aspirations: both utopia and economic opportunity proved elusive, the former far more than the latter.

3. Another recurrent theme of the chapter is the tension between religious idealism and violence. The colonial world was a violent one, both in contact with the Native Americans and in the social conflicts that emerged in the difficult early years of settlement.

4. The English colonists not only clashed with Native American cultures but also developed different cultures themselves. This chapter is structured

around the reconstruction of the modes of settlement and character of life in five distinctly different societies along the Atlantic Coast: the Chesapeake region of Virginia and Maryland, Puritan New England, New York under the Dutch and English, Proprietary Carolina, and Quaker Pennsylvania. In the account of each society is a picture of daily life as reflected in the architecture of houses, material household belongings, patterns of family life, and the role of women.

(3) LEARNING GOALS

Familiarity with Basic Knowledge

After reading this chapter, you should be able to:

1. Locate the various distinct settlements on a map of the Atlantic Coast, in particular Jamestown and the Chesapeake Bay tobacco area, Roanoke Island, Charleston, Plymouth, Boston and Massachusetts Bay, New York, the Hudson River, Delaware, the Connecticut and James rivers, and Philadelphia and the greater Pennsylvania settlement.

2. Describe the changing population, social patterns, and daily life of the Chesapeake tobacco coast in the seventeenth century.

3. Describe the beliefs, social patterns, and the character of village life of the New England Puritans in England in early seventeenth-century Massachusetts.

4. Outline the major features of economic and social life in seventeenth-century New York and Carolina.

5. Describe Quaker beliefs and the efforts to build a peaceable kingdom in William Penn's settlement in Pennsylvania.

Practice in Historical Thinking Skills

After reading this chapter, you should be able to:

1. Compare and contrast the reasons and motivations for the settlement of each of the five main colonies, and describe the relationship of each of the five settlements with the Native American Indians of that region.

22

2. Reconstruct and compare the essentials of daily life, including the lives of women, in each of the five settlements in the seventeenth century.

3. Discuss whether you think utopian idealism or economic necessity was a more important motivation in the settlement and development of the English colonies.

(4) IMPORTANT DATES AND NAMES TO KNOW

1590	Roanoke Island colony fails
1604-1609	Samuel de Champlain establishes fur trading stations in French Canada
1607	Jamestown settled
1616-1621	Native American population in New England decimated by European diseases
1617	First tobacco crop shipped from Virginia
1619	First blacks arrive in Jamestown
1620	Pilgrims land at Plymouth
1622	Powhatan tribes attack Virginia settlements
1624	Dutch colonize mouth of Hudson River
1630	Puritan migration to Massachusetts Bay
1632	Maryland grant to Lord Baltimore (George Calvert)
1633-1634	Native Americans in New England again struck by European diseases
1635	Roger Williams banished to Rhode Island
1636	Anne Hutchinson exiled to Rhode Island
1637	New England wages war against the Pequot Indians
1640	English Civil War ends great migration to New England
1643	Confederation of New England
1659	Two Quaker men hanged on Boston Common

1660	Restoration of King Charles II
1663	Carolina charter granted to eight proprietors
1664	English capture New Netherland and rename it New Yo Royal grant of the Jersey lands to proprietors
1681	William Penn receives Pennsylvania grant

Other Names to Know

Captain John Smith	Opechancanough
Powhatan	William Bradford
John Winthrop	George Fox

(5) GLOSSARY OF IMPORTANT TERMS

indentured servants: European migrants, usually young and single, who entered into work contracts for a specified period of years in exchange for free passage to the New World and sometimes a promise of land at the end of the contract

proprietors: prominent Englishmen to whom the king granted vast areas of land in the New World

antinomianism: an interpretation of Puritan doctrine associated with Anne Hutchinson that stressed mystical elements in God's grace and diverged from orthodox Puritan views on salvation

Puritans: English Protestants who wished not only to purify the Church of England but also to reform English society; they came to New England to set up a model community as an example to England

Pilgrims: a radical separatist group of English Protestants who settled at Plymouth in order to be left alone to lead a pure and primitive life

Society of Friends (Quakers): a visionary radical sect, much persecuted, whose members believed, among other things, in an inner light that brought them close to God, equality in religious and social life, pacifism, and defiance of authority when it denied their right to practice their religion

24

magistrates: secular, civil leaders in Massachusetts Bay, usually not ministers

(6) ENRICHMENT IDEAS

1. As an extension of the RTP in this chapter, recall the differences in housing between Massachusetts Bay and the Chesapeake region. How do the houses and their furnishings show the differences and similarities in the two societies? Find examples of house design in Maryland and Virginia in the early eighteenth century. What are the significant differences between the earlier Chesapeake housing and these? What do the newer designs reveal about social and economic changes? You can also compare the Boardmen house to eighteenth-century Massachusetts houses to see what kind of changes have taken place there.

2. As a class project, make replicas or plans of typical villages from each settlement. This can include everything from designs on paper to miniature villages on tabletops fashioned out of Popsicle sticks and the like. Note how house designs reflect daily life in the different settlements.

3. Write a letter or diary entry describing the daily life of a typical inhabitant on a typical day in three or four of the five settlements in seventeenth-century America.

4. Construct an imaginary document reflecting each settlement's attitude toward and relationship with the area's Indian tribes. The document might be a sermon, a treaty, a leader's policy statement, a letter by a young man or woman in the settlement, or a speech (or letter) by a young Indian of the appropriate area.

5. Imagine yourself to be an indentured servant in the Chesapeake. Were you to write a letter home to a brother or sister, how would you describe your life? Would you encourage your brother or sister to come to the New World?

(7) SAMPLE TEST AND EXAMINATION QUESTIONS

Multiple choice: Choose the best answer.

1. The Jamestown colony suffered all of the following problems of population except

    B
    a. too few skilled workers
    b. too many gold-seeking gentlemen
    c. too many slaves
    d. too few women

2. Most indentured servants who came to Virginia and Maryland in the seventeenth century were

    B
    a. married couples
    b. young, single, and male
    c. young, single, and female
    d. black Africans

3. Houses in the Chesapeake region were

    A
    a. crude, one-room structures
    b. large homes with sleeping lofts and lean-to kitchens
    c. small predecessors of plantation-style houses
    d. connected to long tobacco-drying barns

4. Women in Chesapeake society, as compared to New England,

    B
    a. died young and were scarce
    b. were given religious freedom
    c. lived long lives, bearing many children
    d. were at the center of both economic and political life

5. Puritans migrated to Massachusetts Bay because they wanted

    a. to convert heathens
    b. religious liberty and purity
    c. to set up an experiment in religious toleration
    d. to be left alone to pursue their vision of a pure religious community

6. Which colony is not matched with its major crop?

    B
    a. Virginia-tobacco
    b. South Carolina-rice
    c. West Indies-bananas
    d. Massachusetts-fish

7. The massacre at Jamestown in 1622
    a. avenged the Pequot massacre in Connecticut
    b. was used as justification by many to make

permanent war on the Indians
c. virtually wiped out the entire English colony
d. was led by a disappointed Powhatan suitor of Pocahontas

8. Roger Williams was a problem for the ruling authorities in Massachusetts Bay primarily because
a. he advocated the separation of church and state
b. he accused the Puritans of illegal intrusion on Indian lands
c. he was too pure and godly
d. all of the above

9. Anne Hutchinson was excommunicated from a Boston church primarily because
a. she preached numerous erroneous theological opinions
b. she incited wives to demand equal rights from their husbands
c. she opposed wage and price controls
d. all of the above

10. New England women
a. played a significant role in deciding church policies
b. died in childbirth at a younger age than European women
c. lived longer and bore more children than the European norm
d. played a significant role in the family-centered society

11. Which is the correct order of settlement?
a. Carolina, Pennsylvania, Maryland, Rhode Island
b. Rhode Island, Pennsylvania, Maryland, Carolina
c. Rhode Island, Maryland, Carolina, Pennsylvania
d. Maryland, Carolina, Rhode Island, Pennsylvania

12. Quakers believed in all of the following except
a. equality of all persons, including women, in religious matters
b. renunciation of the use of force in human affairs
c. renunciation of making money as an affront to God
d. no church leaders or institutions standing between an individual and God

13. The most harmonious relations between English colonists and Native American Indians were found in
a. Pennsylvania
b. Carolina
c. Massachusetts Bay
d. Virginia

14. The pattern of the Quaker dispersal into rural
    Pennsylvania was to settle
    a. in compact towns, as in New England
    b. in closely-knit Quaker kinship groups from the
        same European regions
    c. in large towns populated by diverse nationality
        groups
    d. as individual families, thus fracturing a sense
        of identity and community

15. According to the chapter author, the foundations for
    pluralism in America were laid in
    a. the Massachusetts pattern of settling new towns
    b. Penn's policies of peaceful relations with the
        Indians
    c. Penn's policies of toleration and open
        immigration
    d. the diversity represented by the various
        settlements along the Atlantic Coast

   Identify and show a relationship between each of the
following pairs:

Virginia	and	Massachusetts Bay Company
meetinghouse	and	town meeting
Captain John Smith	and	Powhatan
Captain John Mason	and	Roger Williams
George Fox	and	Mary Dyer
John Winthrop	and	William Bradford
William Penn	and	New Netherland

   [This question form, which invites a short essay, com-
bines a basic memory task (identifying the person or term)
with a higher-order thinking skill (showing a connection).
Note that the instruction says "a" relationship, not "the"
relationship, suggesting that there is no single "right
answer." There are many possible connections, but in the
following examples each new answer is better than the last:
Captain Mason and Roger Williams were "both Puritans"; they
were both Puritans who left Massachusetts Bay to start other
colonies; they were both Puritans who left Massachusetts Bay
for different reasons, one willingly and the other banished;
they were both Puritans who left Massachusetts Bay to found
new colonies and who had different attitudes toward the
Indians--Mason massacred them and Williams befriended them.]

Essays

1. Compare and contrast the social patterns of life in the Chesapeake area, New England, and Pennsylvania.

2. The character of immigration to the Chesapeake, Massachusetts Bay, the Carolinas, and Pennsylvania goes a long way toward explaining the social development of each place. Discuss with evidence.

3. Why do you think utopian perfectionism proved to be so elusive for colonial Americans? To what extent do you think the answer is found in human nature or in historical conditions?

Identify and Interpret: Quotation
(that is, state who, what, where, when, and why significant)

We must be knit together in this work as one man. We must entertain each other in brotherly affection. . . . We must delight in each other, make others' conditions our own, rejoice together, mourn together, labor and suffer together: always having before our eyes our commission and community in the work, our community as members of the same body. . . . We shall find that the God of Israel is among us, when ten of us shall be able to resist a thousand of our enemies, when He shall make us a praise and glory, that men shall say of succeeding plantations: "The Lord make it like that of New England." For we must consider that we shall be as a city upon a hill, the eyes of all people are upon us.

3

Mastering the New World

(1) CHAPTER OUTLINE

Anthony and Mary Johnson, two freed slaves, live in the uneasy world between freedom and slavery. Although the family initially prospers, as attitudes toward blacks harden they find fewer and fewer opportunities available to them. The Johnson children and grandchildren are unable to match the modest success of Anthony and Mary.

Black Bondage

> The Slave Trade
> The Southern Transition to Black Labor
> Slavery in the Northern Colonies
> The System of Bondage

Slave Culture

> The Growth of Slavery
> Resistance and Rebellion
> Black Religion and Family

The Struggle for Land

> King Philip's War in New England
> Bacon's Rebellion Engulfs Virginia

An Era of Instability

    Organizing the Empire
    The Glorious Revolution in New England
    Leisler's Rebellion in New York
    Southern Rumblings
    The Social Basis of Politics
    Witchcraft in Salem

Contending for a Continent

    Anglo-French Rivalry
    The Results of War

Conclusion: Controlling the New Environment

(2) SIGNIFICANT THEMES AND HIGHLIGHTS

1. This chapter treats five conflicts in the colonial period between 1675 and 1715: two dealt with the European colonial effort to establish mastery over African slaves and Native American Indians; two concerned administrative and class struggles among the English colonists themselves; the final one was an international struggle as the British sought mastery over French, Dutch, and Spanish colonial contenders.

2. Although the boundaries of American slavery were at first fluid, as the Johnsons' experience showed, the institution of slavery altered the shape of American society. Slavery became a primary source of labor and profits in the Chesapeake but was also closely bound up with economic life in the North. Slavery profoundly affected the lives of both white and black Americans and was an ironic comment on the dream of America as a place of refuge and hope. The personal stories of Olaudah Equiano, and the Johnson clan convey some of the pain connected with slavery and the status of blacks.

3. At the same time that racial boundaries between blacks and whites were hardening, the violent battle of whites for Native American lands continued. The struggle is described in New England, the Chesapeake, and South Carolina. Although losses were heavy for both Native Americans and white settlers, in the end, the coastal tribes were defeated.

4. Small insurrections against colonial administrators and elites, triggered by the Glorious Revolution of 1688, erupted in several colonies. Although they were in no way a "dress rehearsal" for the American Revolution, they did reveal some of the social and political tensions growing out of the attempt to plant English society in the New World.

5. Soon after these insurrections, Europe plunged into war. Rivalries of the Old World affected the New even though the major battlefields were, in fact, far away from the colonies. The impact of European events on the colonies is another indication of the close bonds between the new society and the old.

(3) LEARNING GOALS

Familiarity with Basic Knowledge

After reading this chapter, you should be able to:

1. Describe the slave trade and explain three ways in which the presence of black slaves altered the direction of American society.

2. Give three reasons for the transformation of the Chesapeake labor force in the late seventeenth century.

3. Describe some features of the culture of African-Americans in the seventeenth century.

4. Describe the course and consequences of King Philip's War in New England and Bacon's Rebellion in Virginia.

5. Outline the steps leading to the Glorious Revolution and briefly explain what it was.

6. State three basic differences between the French and English settlements in North America.

Practice in Historical Thinking Skills

After reading this chapter, you should be able to:

1. Analyze how the conflicts between Englishmen and Africans and Native Americans, among Englishmen themselves, and between the British and other European nations changed the relations among white, black, and red people in the New World.

2.   Show the most important effects of the Glorious
     Revolution in England and of European national
     rivalries on the colonies in the late seventeenth and
     early eighteenth centuries.

3.   Explain why the late seventeenth century has been
     described as a period of great instability and change
     in American history.

(4) IMPORTANT DATES AND NAMES TO KNOW

1600-1700	Dutch monopolize slave trade
1619	First Africans imported to Virginia
1637	Pequot War in New England
1640s	New England merchants enter slave trade Virginia forbids blacks to carry firearms
1650-1670	Judicial and legislative decisions in the Chesapeake solidify racial lines
1660	Parliament passes first Navigation Act
1664	English conquer New Netherland
1673-1685	French expand into Mississippi valley
1675-1677	King Philip's War
1676	Bacon's Rebellion in Virginia
1682	LaSalle sails down Mississippi River and claims Louisiana for France
1684	Massachusetts charter recalled
1686	Dominion of New England
1688	Glorious Revolution in England, followed by accession of William and Mary
1689	Overthrow of Governor Edmund Andros in New England Leisler's Rebellion in New York
1690	Transition from white indentured to black slave labor begins in Chesapeake

33

1689-1697	King William's War
1692	Witchcraft crisis in Salem
1702-1713	Queen Anne's War
1713	Peace of Utrecht

Other Names to Know

Sir William Berkeley
Metacomet

Andrew Belcher
William Phips

(5) GLOSSARY OF IMPORTANT TERMS

black codes: laws borrowed from the English colonists in the Caribbean that severely limited black rights and activities

miscegenation: sexual union between members of different races

genocide: the willed extermination of a race or ethnic group by another

Glorious Revolution: the English revolution of 1688 that replaced James II with William and Mary. The revolution was based on the rejection of the "divine right" of kings and was a victory for Protestants, parliamentary power, and the English merchant and gentry class

(6) ENRICHMENT IDEAS

1. After working with the questions in the RTP about how tombstones reveal changing attitudes, especially toward religion, design some tombstones of your own, including both epitaph (inscription) and iconography (pictorial design). Make one or two for the mid-seventeenth century and one or two for the early eighteenth century. Finally, design a modern tombstone, perhaps for yourself or a friend, showing how epitaphs and iconography reflect contemporary attitudes and values.

34

2. Chart the main events in Anthony Johnson's life and
    the lives of his children. Then try to imagine how
    Anthony would explain each of the most important
    events. How might he explain the changing nature of
    race relations? What advice would you give to
    Johnson and his family?

3. In what ways does this chapter suggest that racism is
    a continuing part of American life? Which came first
    in American society, racism or slavery? What
    relevance does this chapter have for today? What
    social or international conflicts still go on between
    peoples?

(7) SAMPLE TEST AND EXAMINATION QUESTIONS

Multiple choice: Choose the best answer.

1. The fewest number of slaves in the seventeenth and
    eighteenth centuries were transported to
    a. the West Indies
    b. North America
    c   Spanish America
    d. Brazil

2. English colonists in the seventeenth century
    a. used black slaves as their main source of labor
    b. depended on Native Americans
    c. found the supply of white indentured servants
        sufficient for their needs
    d. needed no outside supply of workers

3. Slavery never became the foundation of the northern
    colonial work force because northerners
    a. had moral objections to it
    b. used hired hands to work their labor-intensive
        crops
    c. did not have any money to buy slaves
    d. had small family farms and did not need slaves

4. Compared to slaves in the rest of the New World,
    slaves in North America
    a. enjoyed a relatively healthy environment
    b. died off quickly because of disease
    c. had little opportunity to develop a culture
        because of their short life span
    d. had little opportunity for family life

35

5. All of the following statements are true about slavery except
   a. a majority of southern slaves in the eighteenth century worked on plantations with at least ten other slaves
   b. slaves were widely dispersed among the northern population
   c. slaves were more frequently found in northern cities than in the countryside
   d. slaves were welcomed by white artisans who had more work than they could do themselves

6. Slave resistance in North America did not usually take the form of
   a. overt rebellion
   b. goldbricking
   c. running away
   d. arson and breaking tools

7. Black Christianity
   a. was drawn primarily from the religion of the master class
   b. blended African religious practices with those of the white church
   c. strongly influenced white religions
   d. rejected the whole idea of Protestant Evangelicalism

8. A major barrier to slave family life was
   a. the imbalance of women to men
   b. white exploitation of black women
   c. polygamy
   d. too many single men

9. The underlying cause of King Philip's War was
   a. the trial and execution of three Wampanoags
   b. young tribesmen's anger over white encroachments on their lands
   c. King Philip's desire for an English wife
   d. all of the above

10. The results of King Philip's War included
    a. the extension of the New England frontier
    b. the rebuilding of all of New England's 90 towns
    c. the devastation of Indian society in New England
    d. the call for colonial unity

11. Bacon's Rebellion involved all of the following issues except
    a. a lack of opportunity for land expansion
    b. declining tobacco prices and rising taxes, which aggravated social-class conflict

36

c. conflict between white frontiersmen and the Susquehannock Indians
d. rivalry between free blacks and indentured servants for land near Williamsburg

12. Sir Edmund Andros outraged New Englanders by
   a. imposing taxes without legislative consent
   b. turning a Congregational church into an Anglican one
   c. establishing freedom of religion
   d. all of the above

13. The Salem witchcraft trials were evidence of
   a. the Devil's plan to destroy Puritanism
   b. an Indian plot to avenge white massacres
   c. the irrationality of teenage girls
   d. none of the above

14. In the period of European rivalry in the late seventeenth and early eighteenth centuries, the colonies
   a. were not at all affected
   b. let the Iroquois do most of the fighting
   c. suffered grievously, especially in New England
   d. split evenly in support of the French and English

15. New France came into conflict with New England primarily because of
   a. religious and commercial rivalry
   b. competition for fertile farmlands
   c. the pressures of population
   d. none of the above

Identify and show a relationship between each of the following pairs:

James II	and	Governor Berkeley
Jacob Leisler	and	Sir Edmund Andros
Nathaniel Bacon	and	King Philip
LaSalle	and	Peace of Utrecht

Essays

1. Explain why the late seventeenth century was a period of great instability and changing relationships in North America.

2. "The history of the colonies in the seventeenth century showed the impossibility of re-creating society on an English model. New conditions and

37

unexpected new forces made it difficult to copy the familiar Old World in the New." Write an essay, using specific material from this chapter, to support this statement.

3. Black slaves faced the same problem of re-creating, or even preserving, cultural forms of their African past in North America. How successful were they in retaining what was familiar to them in the new conditions they found in the Americas? Support your answer with evidence drawn from this chapter.

4. Discuss four conflicts among different peoples and nations in the New World between 1675 and 1715.

Identify and Interpret: Chart

(that is, first, study the chart and describe what it shows; second, analyze the chart by explaining some of the reasons behind the patterns you see; third, assess the larger significance of the chart)

GROWTH OF THE COLONIAL POPULATION: WHITE AND BLACK

	Estimated Total	White	Black	(Black as % of Tot
1640	26,634	26,037	596	(2%)
1670	111,935	107,400	4,535	(4%)
1700	250,888	223,071	27,817	(11%)
1740	905,563	755,539	150,024	(16.5%)
1770	2,148,076	1,688,254	459,822	(21%)

Source: U.S. Bureau of Census.

4

The Maturing of Colonial Society

(1) CHAPTER OUTLINE

During a period of rapid growth, Devereaux Jarratt grows up in the family of a Virginia yeoman farmer. His interest in books and learning enables him to become a tutor for rich Virginia planter families. Eventually he rises to become an Anglican clergyman.

America's First Population Explosion

> The New Immigrants
> New Classes of Newcomers
> A Land of Opportunity?
> Africans in Chains

Beyond the Appalachians

> Cultural Changes Among Interior Tribes
> France's Inland Empire
> Spain's America

A Land of Family Farms

> Northern Agricultural Society
> Changing Values
> Women in Northern Colonial Society

The Plantation South

> The Tobacco Coast
> The Rice Coast
> The Backcountry
> Family Life in the South

The Urban World of Commerce and Ideas

> Sinews of Trade
> The Artisans' World
> Urban Social Structure
> The Entrepreneurial Ethos
> The American Enlightenment

The Great Awakening

> Fading Faith
> The Awakeners' Message
> The Urban North
> The Rural South
> Legacy of the Awakening

Political Life

> Structuring Colonial Governments
> The Crowd in Action
> The Growing Power of the Assemblies
> Local Politics
> The Spread of Whig Ideology

Conclusion: America in 1750

(2) SIGNIFICANT THEMES AND HIGHLIGHTS

1. In the first half of the eighteenth century, America
    was made up of several distinct regional societies,
    each in the process of growth and change. Beyond the
    Appalachians, extensive contact with France's growing
    inland empire and Spanish American settlements in the
    South and Southwest transformed Native American ways
    of life. English settlements, however, exploding in
    population, threatened Indian cultural cohesion the
    most. This chapter stresses the increasing
    complexity, adaption, and maturing of colonial
    English society. The eighteenth century provided
    opportunities for some, like Devereaux Jarratt, great
    gains for a few, like Boston merchant Andrew Belcher,
    but disappointment and privation for many others.

40

2. The farming society of the North was characterized by widespread land ownership and a rough kind of economic equality. In the South, plantation society was marked by the emergence of a gentry class and a labor force almost entirely made up of black slaves, while the backcountry, still in the frontier stages and settled by thousands of Scots-Irish and German immigrants, lacked the sharp class distinctions of the tidewater region. Colonial cities, with their highly differentiated class structure and new commercial values, were on the "cutting edge" of change. In each area, women played an important but limited role in daily life.

3. The Great Awakening was more than a religious revival, for it produced patterns of thought and behavior that helped to fuel the Revolution. The course of the Great Awakening in Boston and Virginia vividly shows the way in which its message fused with local social and economic tensions to threaten established authority.

4. Although many historians focus on the changing political arrangements in the colonies in the first half of the eighteenth century as a means of preparing for a discussion of the Revolution, this chapter makes the point that the fluidity of American society itself must be understood as a prelude to the events of the 1770s.

(3) LEARNING GOALS

Familiarity with Basic Knowledge

After reading this chapter, you should be able to:

1. Name the major immigrant groups coming to the colonies in the early eighteenth century, describe their social background, find their destinations on the map, and summarize their relative opportunities for social and economic advancement.

2. Describe the cultural changes of the interior Indian tribes as a result of their contact with French, Spanish, and English settlements on economic, social, and domestic life; on their relation to the environment; on political organization; and on intertribal tensions.

41

3. Describe northern farm society and its most important social characteristics and problems, including family life and the ways in which the roles and rights of women changed in the colonies.

4. Give an account of the "profound social transition" of the Upper South, characterize the social and political nature of the southern gentry, and detail the social and economic differences between the tobacco and rice coasts and the backcountry.

5. Describe the urban social structure, including the merchant's pivotal role, and the work pattern and attitudes of urban artisans.

6. Explain the major events and message of the Great Awakening, including its comparative impact on new England and the southern colonies and its effects on colonial political life.

Practice in Historical Thinking Skills

After reading this chapter, you should be able to:

1. Compare and contrast the development and maturing of English society in the farming northern colonies, in the plantation South, and in colonial cities.

2. Discuss the foundations of colonial political structures and ideology, including what colonists meant by a political balance of power and how it matched the reality of Whig ideology and local political arrangements.

3. Analyze how the kaleidoscopic mixture of ethnic, racial, religious, and regional settlements in North America, as well as class differences, provided awkward incongruities and threats of social unrest in the various societies of the New World.

(4) IMPORTANT DATES AND NAMES TO KNOW

1662   Half-Way Covenant in New England

1685   Beginning of 30-year stagnation in the tobacco marke

1704   Boston News-Letter, first colonial newspaper, published

42

1713	Beginning of Scots-Irish and German immigration
1715-1730	Volume of slave trade doubles
1718	French settle New Orleans
1720s	Black population begins to increase naturally
1734-1736	Great Awakening begins in Northampton, Massachusetts
1735	Zenger acquitted of seditious libel in New York
1739-40	Whitefield's first American tour spreads Great Awakening Slaves compose 90 percent of population on Carolina rice coast
1740s	Indigo becomes staple crop in Lower South
1747	Benjamin Franklin publishes first Poor Richard's Almanack Impressment riot in Boston
1760	Africans compose 20 percent of American population
1760s-1770s	Spanish establish California mission system
1769	American Philosophical Society founded at Philadelphia

Other Names to Know

Jonathan Edwards
Gilbert Tennent
Cesar Ghiselin
Francis Richardson

Benjamin Franklin
James Davenport
Thomas Hancock

(5) GLOSSARY OF IMPORTANT TERMS

artisan: a skilled worker, using hand tools, usually in a small shop, such as a carpenter, shoemaker, or silversmith

Half-Way Covenant: an attempt by New England clergy in 1662 to counteract declining church membership by allowing the children of church members to join the church even though they had not experienced salvation; they were, however, denied voting and communion rights

<u>franchise:</u> the right to vote, widespread among colonial free
    white males

<u>power of the purse:</u> the power of colonial legislatures in
    the eighteenth century to initiate money bills,
    specifying the amount to be raised and its uses

(6) ENRICHMENT IDEAS

1. Find and examine other tax lists than the ones in the
    RTP to see how they reveal inequalities of wealth.
    Look at (or imagine) the tax records for the citizens
    of your hometown today to see how they continue to
    shed light on the distribution of wealth.

2. If you live in the East, you will probably be able to
    visit a historic house that dates from this period.
    In the South, see the country houses of the new
    gentry class or their town houses in Williamsburg.
    In the North and the Mid-Atlantic states, there are
    fine old houses of the merchant class and often of
    German immigrants. What do the houses suggest about
    daily life and about the class structure of the
    eighteenth century? Do you see evidences of slaves
    or servants? What suggestions are there about the
    lives of women and children? What would you conclude
    about the nature of work and leisure? Does the
    historic preservation of a house present a
    romanticized version of life in the past?

3. Consider recent episodes of religious revivalism.
    What has changed and what is the same?

4. Does the existence of pluralistic ethnic, racial,
    religious, and regional groups strengthen or threaten
    American cultural and political life today?

(7) SAMPLE TEST AND EXAMINATION QUESTIONS

Multiple choice: Choose the best answer.

1. Which of the following correctly arranges the immigrant group in terms of size in the eighteenth century (largest first):
   a. Africans, Scots-Irish, Germans, Swiss
   b. Germans, Africans, Scots-Irish, Swiss
   c. Scots-Irish, Germans, Swiss, Africans
   d. Africans, Germans, Scots-Irish, Swiss

2. The fastest-growing area in the early eighteenth century was
   a. New England
   b. South Carolina
   c. the northern frontier
   d. the area south from Pennsylvania

3. Most eighteenth-century emigrants were
   a. wealthy landed aristocrats
   b. middle-class artisans and yeoman farmers
   c. slaves and indentured servants
   d. prisoners

4. Most eighteenth-century indentured servants
   a. died or ran away before their time of service was over
   b. were brought from Africa
   c. usually were able to buy land after serving their time
   d. completed their time but rarely became independent property owners

5. Contact with the European colonists changed all of the following Indian cultural characteristics except
   a. their matrilineal family life and clear division of work roles
   b. their local political organization
   c. their spiritual relation to the environment
   d. their system of law and justice and basic family organization

6. Northern farming society was characterized by
   a. a small class of rich, large farmers
   b. large numbers of poverty-stricken farmers
   c. widespread ownership of moderate-size farms
   d. a large renter class

7. Colonial American women in the eighteenth century
    a. rarely married for love
    b. could get divorced if their marriages failed
    c. had limited but significant responsibilities in
        their families and neighborhoods
    d. forfeited all property rights when they married

8. All of the following statements describe the Upper
    South tobacco coast in the eighteenth century except
    a. slaves replaced indentured servants as the labor
        force
    b. agriculture became more diversified
    c. single white males still outnumbered white women
    d. a majority of families owned no slaves

9. In the backcountry of the South, settlers
    a. were German and Scots-Irish
    b. pursued mixed farming and cattle raising
    c. had few institutions
    d. all of the above

10. In the eighteenth century, what percentage of
    Americans lived in cities?
    a. 5 percent
    b. 10 percent
    c. 15 percent
    d. 20 percent

11. Urban artisans
    a. easily expected a rapid rise to ownership of
        their own shops
    b. took fierce pride in themselves as community
        leaders
    c. viewed themselves as "mere mechanics"
    d. read Ben Franklin's Poor Richard's Almanack
        regularly for advice

12. All of the following statements about eighteenth-
    century cities are true except that they
    a. showed an increasing gap between rich and poor
    b. showed evidence of a new entrepreneurial ethic
    c. were marked by episodes of intensely violent
        social conflict
    d. devised new ways of dealing with the poor

13. In the early eighteenth century, most Americans
    a. were Congregationalists
    b. were Anglicans
    c. were Baptists
    d. belonged to no church at all

14. The Great Awakening
    a. decreased the number of religious sects
    b. undermined church-state ties
    c. led to the notion that community unity was attainable
    d. encouraged higher education by emphasizing that the clergy should be educated in the established church

15. American political assumptions included the belief that
    a. only free men with property should vote
    b. only men of wealth and social status should hold positions of political power
    c. people had the right to protest openly if power was abused
    d. all of the above

16. In the mid-eighteenth century, colonial assemblies
    a. gradually gained more powers, such as that of initiating money bills
    b. were mainly advisory bodies
    c. were regularly dissolved by royal governors
    d. ignored instructions from local constituencies

Essays

1. The three items under "Practice in Historical Thinking Skills" can serve as the basis for essays.

2. The Great Awakening transformed American life and thought in significant ways. Support this statement using appropriate evidence.

3. Rising tensions among social classes characterized colonial society in the eighteenth century and made political and religious struggles bitter. Discuss with evidence.

Identify and Interpret: Quotation
(that is, state who, what, where, when, and why significant)

The bow of God's wrath is bent, and the arrow made ready on the string; and justice bends the arrow at your heart, and strains the bow; and it is nothing but the mere pleasure of God, and that of an angry God, without any promise or obligation at all, that keeps the arrow one moment from being made drunk with your blood. Thus are all you that never passed under a great change of heart, by the mighty power of the Spirit of God upon your souls; all you that were never born again, and made new creatures. . . The God that holds you over the pit of hell, much as one holds a spider or some loathsome insect over the fire, abhors you, and is dreadfully provoked; his wrath towards you burns like fire; he looks upon you as worthy of nothing else, but to be cast into the fire.

5

Bursting the Colonial Bonds

(1) CHAPTER OUTLINE

Shoemaker Ebenezer MacIntosh finds that the Stamp Act crisis offers him opportunities for influence and prominence. He leads mobs during the Stamp Act crisis protesting against both English authority and Boston's elite.

The Climactic Seven Year's War

> War and the Management of Empire
> Outbreak of Hostilities
> Tribal Strategies
> Consequences of War

The Crisis with England

> Sugar, Currency, and Stamps
> Stamp Act Riots
> An Uncertain Interlude
> The Growing Rift
> The Final Rupture

The Ideology of Revolutionary Republicanism

> A Plot Against Liberty
> Rejecting Monarchy
> Balancing Liberty and Power
> Debate over Political Equality

The Turmoil of Revolutionary Society

>   Urban People
>   Protesting Farmers

Conclusion: Forging a Revolution

(2) SIGNIFICANT THEMES AND HIGHLIGHTS

1. Beginning with Ebenezer MacIntosh, the chapter
    stresses the role of common people in the events
    leading to the American Revolution rather than
    placing the usual emphasis on famous founding
    fathers.

2. The chapter shows that there was widespread group
    support for not one but two American revolutions. As
    MacIntosh's activities suggest, the "dual American
    Revolution" combined an external struggle to sever
    colonial ties to England with an internal struggle
    for control and reform of colonial society. The
    colonists sought liberation from English rule. But
    they also sought to combat the aristocratic, elitist
    nature of colonial society. The first revolution,
    marked by violent conflict with England, was the War
    for American Independence; the second, which involved
    intense class resentments, is called the American
    Revolution. The first ended in the Declaration of
    Independence; the second continued long into the next
    century.

3. The chapter not only explains these two revolutions
    but also interweaves colonial history with events in
    Europe and with the Native American tribes of the
    interior forests. The perspectives, survival
    strategies, and cultural changes of the Iroquois,
    Creek, and Cherokee are seen to be just as important
    as those of the British, French, and American
    colonists. The harmful effects of the Seven Years War
    loom large in this chapter, especially on groups like
    the urban laboring poor, backcountry farmers, and
    women.

4. These groups each had their own struggles against
    concentrated wealth and power. But these differences
    were fruitful, for with educated lawyers and rich
    merchants and planters they fashioned a political
    ideology of revolutionary republicanism.

(3) LEARNING GOALS

Familiarity with Basic Knowledge

After reading this chapter, you should be able to:

1. Make a clear statement distinguishing between the War for American Independence and the American Revolution.

2. Describe the issues at stake in the series of wars of empire between England, Spain, France, and the several Native American Indian tribes, and outline the major developments and consequences of the Seven Years' War.

3. Outline the steps in the crisis with England between 1763 and 1776 leading to the War for American Independence.

4. Explain the essential issues and elements involved in the ideology of revolutionary republicanism.

5. Describe the grievances and concerns of ordinary Americans between 1763 and 1776, explaining how urban people, women, and farmers understood their "liberties" and "natural rights" in the early 1770s.

Practice in Historical Thinking Skills

After reading this chapter, you should be able to:

1. Discuss the two revolutions going on in the British colonies between 1763 and 1776, explaining the main characteristics of each and indicating which revolution you think motivated the American people more in the 1760s and 1770s.

2. Assess the mutual impact and influence of the interior Indian tribes, the American colonists, and the British and French on one another in the mid-eighteenth century.

3. Identify the chapter author's interpretation of "the nature of the American Revolution" and cite the evidence presented to support that point of view.

(4) IMPORTANT DATES AND NAMES TO KNOW

1696	Board of Trade established
1701	Iroquois establish policy of neutrality
1702-1713	Queen Anne's War
1713	Peace of Utrecht
1733	Molasses Act
1744-1748	King George's War
1754	Albany Congress convened
1755	Braddock defeated by French and Indian allies
1756-1763	Seven Years' War
1759	Wolfe defeats the French at Quebec
1759-1761	Cherokee War against the English
1760s	Economic Slump
1763	Treaty of Paris ends Seven Years' War Proclamation line limits westward expansion
1764	Sugar and Currency acts Pontiac's Rebellion in Ohio valley
1765	Stamp Act Stamp Act Congress and resistance
1766	Declaratory Act Tenant rent war in New York Slave insurrections in South Carolina
1767	Townshend duties imposed
1768	British troops occupy Boston
1770	"Boston massacre" Townshend duties repealed (except on tea)
1771	Carolina Regulators defeated
1772	Gaspee incident in Rhode Island

1773	Tea Act provokes Boston Tea Party
1774	"Intolerable Acts" First Continental Congress meets
1775	Second Continental Congress meets Battles of Lexington and Concord
1776	Tom Paine publishes Common Sense Declaration of Independence

Other Names to Know

General James Wolfe
William Pitt
Patrick Henry
John Adams
General Thomas Gage
Governor Thomas Hutchinson

Pontiac
George Grenville
Lord North
Samuel Adams
Andrew Oliver

(5) GLOSSARY OF IMPORTANT TERMS

privateers: privately outfitted ships licensed by colonial governments to attack French shipping during the Seven Years' War

nonimportation and nonconsumption agreements: economic boycotts, as individual colonists pledged neither to import nor to use any British articles but rather to go without or to make their own, the main tactic of colonists protesting the Townshend duties and the Tea Act

revolutionary republicanism: a set of political ideals developed in the American revolutionary era that emphasized anti-monarchy, liberty in balance with power, and political equality in tension with rule by an aristocracy of talent

(6) ENRICHMENT IDEAS

1. Study again the RTP for this chapter, noting how the inventories contribute to your understanding of the class tensions and internal social struggle that was part of the American Revolution.

2. If you live in a rural area or small town (especially in the Midwest), it is likely that your local newspaper will advertise several auctions of the property and household belongings of family farms in the process of dissolution. Go to an auction or two, and note how the items for sale reflect social class.

3. If you live in the East, you can visit such Revolutionary sites as Philadelphia, Boston, and Lexington and Concord, as well as battle sites at Bunker Hill (Breed's Hill), Saratoga, Trenton, Valley Forge, Brandywine, and Yorktown. What interpretation is provided at these sites? Which "American Revolution" is presented? Is there any indication of the social tensions of the inner war? How do you explain the approach taken at these Revolutionary-era sites?

(7) SAMPLE TEST AND EXAMINATION QUESTIONS

Multiple choice: Choose the best answer.

1. In seeking to survive the wars of empire in North America, the Native American Indian tribes
   a. depended on French friendship
   b. formed treaty alliances with the more numerous British
   c. pursued aggressive neutrality in which they shifted their allegiance between the British and the French
   d. formed intertribal confederacies

2. Most at stake for the European powers in the wars of empire was
   a. the economic and political value of North American land and resources
   b. religious freedom
   c. national pride
   d. treaty obligations to the Indians

3. The Seven Years' War
   a. spurred colonial prosperity
   b. required heavy taxes
   c. rendered the colonies vulnerable to fluctuations in the British economy
   d. all of the above

54

4. The British finally turned the tide of battle to
   their side in the Seven Years' War when they
   a. pursued William Pitt's policies in North America
   b. defeated the Iroquois allies of the French
   c. convinced the American colonists to share more of
      the fighting burdens of the war
   d. dispatched General Braddock to attack French
      forts

5. After the Treaty of Paris, economic prosperity in the
   colonies
   a. surged because of captured French resources
   b. turned to depression, especially among the
      laboring classes in coastal towns
   c. remained high because of war profiteering
   d. was largely unchanged

6. The Stamp Act riots
   a. hardened the British attitude toward the colonies
   b. revealed how united all American classes were in
      opposing British authority
   c. politicized the American people against both
      English rule and internal elites
   d. convinced Parliament to limit its authority over
      the colonies

7. The Sugar Act
   a. doubled duties on sugar imported from the West
      Indies
   b. kept duties the same but improved enforcement
   c. cut duties in half but improved enforcement
   d. required stamps on every gallon of imported
      molasses

8. In the early 1770s, a proposal that deeply threatened
   and angered the colonists was one
   a. to tax window glass
   b. to have the British government rather than
      colonial assemblies pay the salaries of royal
      governors
   c. to limit town meetings to once a month
   d. to close the port of Boston permanently

9. Which is in the correct chronological order?
   a. Tea Act, Tea Party, Continental Congress,
      Intolerable Acts
   b. Tea Act, Intolerable Acts, Tea Party, Continental
      Congress
   c. Tea Act, Tea Party, Intolerable Acts, Continental
      Congress
   d. Intolerable Acts, Continental Congress, Tea Act,

Tea Party

10. In the face of tougher expressions of British
    authority, by the end of 1774 the colonists had
    a. knuckled under to British rule
    b. created armed militia units to harass British
       troops and bully local loyalist merchants
    c. sought aid from the French
    d. begun electing their own provincial assemblies to
       draft declarations of independence

11. The ideology of revolutionary republicanism included
    all of the following except
    a. the rejection of monarchy
    b. concern over the dangers of governmental power
    c. a balance between liberty and power
    d. pure levelling political equality

12. Revolutionary agitation for equality and rights among
    social groups was expressed by all of the following
    except
    a. urban artisans
    b. backcountry farmers
    c. Virginia planters
    d. women

13. The dual American Revolution
    a. united all colonial classes in a common effort
    b. exposed class tensions in the process of
       struggling against British tyranny
    c. tore the colonies apart
    d. put the colonists at war with both the French and
       British

14. The Declaration of Independence
    a. was a novel departure from the rhetoric of
       patriotic pamphlets and congressional addresses
    b. was the original brainchild of Thomas Jefferson
    c. was hotly debated by the Continental Congress
    d. was filled with familiar ideas from the
       colonists' British heritage

15. Energy for the American Revolution came from all of
    the following except
    a. Anglican ministers from New York
    b. some wealthy Virginia planters and New England
       merchants
    c. urban artisans in Boston
    d. small farmers in western North Carolina

Identify and show a relationship between each of the following pairs.

Pontiac	and	Proclamation Line of 1763
"Liberty Tree"	and	Andrew Oliver
Thomas Hutchinson	and	Samuel Adams
William Pitt	and	Fort Duquesne
James Wolfe	and	Thomas Gage
George Grenville	and	Patrick Henry
John Hancock	and	Ebenezer MacIntosh
Sons of Liberty	and	Philadelphia militia
Stamp Act	and	Townshend Acts

Essays

1. Items 1-3 under "Practice in Historical Thinking Skills" in the "Learning Goals" section can be used as practice essay questions.

2. To ignore the role of Native Americans in the pre-revolutionary era is to ignore a very real factor in the coming struggle. Discuss with suitable evidence.

3. Even with better will and more compromises on both sides, it would have been difficult to prevent the American War for Independence. It was, in short, inevitable. The "American Revolution," however, was not. Discuss.

4. It has been said that "the American Revolution was not made but prevented." Discuss what you think this means and the extent to which you agree.

Map Question:

Locate the following on the accompanying map.

1. Lake Champlain
2. Iroquois Confederacy
3. Cherokee nation
4. Ohio River valley
5. Fort Duquesne
6. New York City
7. Philadelphia

8. Charleston, South Carolina
9. Fort Ticonderoga
10. Creek nation
11. Jamestown
12. Fort Niagara
13. Boston
14. Quebec City

PART TWO

A REVOLUTIONARY PEOPLE
1 7 7 6 – 1 8 2 8

6

A People in Revolution

(1) CHAPTER OUTLINE

"Long Bill" Scott, wounded and captured by the British, explains that the ambition to better himself rather than patriotism led him to join the Revolutionary army. Still, in the next few years, he escapes twice from the British, fights in New York and Rhode Island, and volunteers for the navy. The main effect of the war for Long Bill and his family, however, was not military exploits but poverty, sickness, and death.

The War for American Independence

     Creating an Independent Government
     The War in the North
     The War Moves South
     Native Americans in the Revolution
     The Devastation of the Iroquois
     Negotiating Peace
     The Ingredients of Victory

The Experience of War

     Recruiting an Army
     The Casualties of Conflict
     Civilians and the War
     The Loyalists
     Blacks and the Revolution

The Revolution and the Economy

> The Interruption of Trade
> Boom and Depression in Agriculture
> Manufacturing and Wartime Profits
> Financial Chaos

The Ferment of Revolutionary Politics

> Politicizing the People
> Mobilizing the People
> The Limits of Citizenship
> Republican Women

Revolutionary Politics in the States

> Creating Republican Governments
> Different Paths to the Republican Goal
> Separating Church and State
> Loyalists and Public Safety
> Slavery Under Attack
> Politics and the Economy

Conclusion: The Crucible of Revolution

(2) SIGNIFICANT THEMES AND HIGHLIGHTS

1. As Long Bill Scott's sad but heroic story reveals, people in America during the Revolution struggled not only to create a nation but even more to improve their own lives. This chapter emphasizes the private struggles and hardships and the disrupted lives of people in America during the Revolutionary War rather than the battles and public policy decisions of the war. The chapter continues the account of class divisions in American society during wartime, which underlines the theme of a "dual revolution."

2. This chapter creates a mood that underlines the startling facts that the American Revolutionary War was the longest war in American history (except one), the most costly in per-capita casualties (except one), and (without exception) the most damaging in terms of per-capita victimization of civilians and the disruption and disarray of economic life.

3. It was in state politics that Americans transformed and expressed the political meaning of the Revolution. The making of new state governments

60

involved converting the ideology of Revolutionary republicanism into action, first by writing state constitutions and second by resolving the thorny issues of Revolutionary times.

4. Although many more ordinary people--white farmers, small shopkeepers, urban artisans, and the like, were politicized and joined the political process, there were limits to republican representation and political participation. Large numbers of Americans-- women, blacks, Indians--were excluded from the new political system. This chapter captures their voice as they express their frustrations with a revolution that stopped short of the full realization of its ideological rhetoric.

(3) LEARNING GOALS

Familiarity with Basic Knowledge

After reading this chapter, you should be able to:

1. Describe the major British and American strategies in the American Revolution and state how well they worked.

2. Explain four or five reasons why the Americans defeated the British and won the war.

3. Describe the economic costs of the war to commerce, agriculture, and manufacturing.

4. Explain how the war affected slaves, Loyalists, and Native American Indians, especially the Iroquois.

5. List the questions that the early republican politicians (or anyone, for that matter) asked when thinking about creating new governments.

6. State a few key differences between the Pennsylvania and Massachusetts state constitutions.

7. State the ways in which Americans were politicized in the Revolutionary era.

Practice in Historical Thinking Skills

After reading this chapter, you should be able to:

1. Analyze how the American people made the shift from separating from an imperial system to the creation of a republican form of government.

2. Assess the extent to which the American Revolution, on balance, was good or bad for slaves, northern farmers, Loyalists, Native Americans, wealthy Patriots, and ordinary citizens.

3. Assess how well Americans were able to fulfill their Revolutionary republican ideology in the war and the postwar era.

(4) IMPORTANT DATES AND NAMES TO KNOW

1775	Continental Congress urges "states" to establish new governments Lord Dunmore's proclamation to slaves and servants in Virginia Congress resolves on Indian friendship Iroquois Six Nations pledge neutrality
1776	British evacuate Boston Declaration of Independence States pass laws against Loyalists Eight states draft constitutions Cherokee raids and American retaliations
1777	British occupy Philadelphia Iroquois join the British (except Tuscarora and Oneida) British surrender at Saratoga Washington's army winters at Valley Forge
1778	People of Massachusetts reject proposed constitution War shifts to the South Savannah falls to the British French Treaty of Alliance and Commerce
1778-1779	Massacres of civilians by Loyalists and Indians German mercenaries spread fear in New Jersey
1779	Sullivan destroys Iroquois villages in New York Massachusetts state constitutional convention

1780	Charleston surrenders to the British
	Nathanael Greene begins partisan warfare in the South
	Pennsylvania begins gradual abolition of slavery
	Massachusetts constitution ratified
1780s	Virginia and Maryland debate abolition of slavery
	Destruction of Iroquois Confederacy
1781	Cornwallis surrenders at Yorktown
	Articles of Confederation ratified by states
1783	Treaty of Paris
	Massachusetts judiciary abolishes slavery
	King's Commission on American Loyalists
1784	Treaty of Fort Stanwix with Iroquois
1785	Treaty of Hopewell with Cherokee
1790	Slave trade outlawed in all states but two

Other Names to Know

General William Howe
Silas Deane
Thomas Danforth
John Adams

Vergennes
Robert Morris
John Dickinson
Thomas Peters

(5) GLOSSARY OF IMPORTANT TERMS

partisan warfare: American strategy (called guerrilla warfare today) under Nathanael Greene in the South whereby several small, highly mobile bands of soldiers waged hit-and-run attacks on British troops rather than standing together as one army

privateering: government chartering of private vessels to prey upon English merchant ships (see glossary for Chapter 5)

bills of credit: paper money issued by the continental government and backed by government credit to finance the war

<u>Loyalists:</u> Americans loyal to the crown during the Revolution who actively supported, sympathized with, or fought on the British side

<u>Sovereignty:</u> Source or locus of ultimate power; for republican ideology, sovereignty resided in the people

(6) ENRICHMENT IDEAS

1. Explore in the RTP the way in which enlistment and muster rolls reveal the social character of Revolutionary War soldiers. Do you think the poor shouldered an unnecessarily heavy burden of the fighting? Interview some veterans of recent American wars, or find studies of the social-class and racial composition of modern soldiers. What do you conclude?

2. If you live in the East, visit Revolutionary War battle sites at Boston, New York, Trenton, Princeton, Bennington, Saratoga, Brandywine, Savannah, Charleston, Cowpens, Guilford Court House, or Yorktown. Imagine yourself a common soldier at one of those battles. Write a letter home or a diary entry describing what it was like.

3. Imagine you are a former Crown official, or a slave, or a New England farmer, or a northern artisan, or a Virginia Patriot slave owner, or a woman living on the frontier, or some other colonist. What reasons would you give to explain your support for or against the war?

4. Difficult material like political ideology is sometimes easier to understand by representing abstract ideas in some sort of visual way. Construct a chart on Revolutionary republican ideology, showing such things as political focus and structures (branches and levels of government), ways of balancing liberty and power, and ideas about equality and who should rule; for example, a continuum:

```
LIBERTY                              POWER/ORDER
-------------------------------------------
HAPPINESS                            PROPERTY

             the  P E O P L E
```

or a diagram showing John Adams's "Thoughts on Government" and his proposal for the Massachusetts state constitution:

LEGISLATIVE		EXECUTIVE	JUDICIARY
REPRESENTATIVE ASSEMBLY	SENATE (Council)	GOVERNOR (President)	
.democratic	.aristocratic	.independent	.separate
.the many	.the few	.the one	and
.liberty	.property	.balancer	distinct

(7) SAMPLE TEST AND EXAMINATION QUESTIONS

Multiple Choice: Choose the best answer.

1. The primary strategy of the American continental forces against the British was
   a. defensive, surviving by avoiding major battles
   b. aggressive, seeking to split British forces in half
   c. to hide while waiting for French help
   d. to let the British have coastal cities while protecting the frontier against Indians

2. All of the following were included in the Treaty of Paris except
   a. the western boundary of the United States was set at the Mississippi River
   b. all debts between citizens of the two countries were invalidated
   c. the British recognized the independence of the United States of America
   d. the Americans promised to restore Loyalists rights and properties

3. The Americans were successful at the Paris treaty convention because
   a. they had the support of the French foreign minister, Vergennes
   b. they ignored the French and negotiated directly with the British
   c. they held Cornwallis hostage until they received generous terms
   d. Franklin and Adams respected instructions from Congress

4. The continental army was made up largely of
   a. poor men conscripted or hired as substitutes by wealthy men in towns filling their quotas
   b. patriotic gentlemen and yeoman farmers
   c. a polygot mixture of local militias
   d. eager volunteer enlisted men

5. Economic costs of the Revolutionary War included all of the following except
   a. rampant inflation
   b. the collapse of the monetary system
   c. the destruction of home manufacturing
   d. the disruption of commerce

6. The American Patriots won the war against Great Britain for all of following reasons except
   a. the administrative talents and determination of General Washington
   b. British caution and lack of will
   c. the enormous drain on England's financial resources
   d. the military skill of the state militias

7. Congress paid for the war by all of the following means except
   a. issuing bills of credit
   b. printing money
   c. levying income taxes
   d. loans from the French and the Dutch

8. Economically, the Revolution
   a. damaged the New England fishing industry
   b. caused trade shifts that opened highly profitable new non-English markets
   c. helped agriculture because the army needed supplies
   d. hurt manufacturing

9. The Iroquois resolve to remain neutral during the Revolution
   a. reflected a new strategy of surviving conflicts among whites in the New World
   b. was abandoned at the Oswego Council when most of the Iroquois nations joined the Patriot cause
   c. resulted in generous land concessions under the Treaty of Paris
   d. was abandoned to side with the British in exchange for trade goods, arms, and protection against expansionist Americans

66

10. The Revolutionary generation agreed that basic to the idea of constitutionalism were all of the following except
   a. constitutions should be written
   b. governments should exist first in order to prepare constitutions
   c. the constitutions were produced by the people
   d. elected rather than appointed representatives were crucial in writing a constitution

11. The Pennsylvania constitution provided for
   a. an executive governor without veto power
   b. two representative legislature
   c. an executive created out of the assembly
   d. no governor

12. The Massachusetts constitution was based on John Adams's ideas of
   a. the predominance of aristocratic power
   b. a weak executive branch
   c. mixed and balanced separate branches of government
   d. power in the lower house

13. The American people were politicized during the American Revolution by
   a. ministers
   b. an outpouring of political pamphlets and newspapers
   c. the frequency of state-level elections
   d. all of the above

Date and put the following events in the correct chronological order:

Lexington and Concord
Boston Tea Party
Treaty of Paris
Stamp Act
Constitutional Convention
Battle of Saratoga
end of Seven Years' War
Declaration of Independence
Yorktown
Treaty of Fort Stanwix

Identify and show a relationship between each of the following pairs:

Treaty of Fort Stanwix	and	Treaty of Hopewell
Silas Deane	and	Robert Morris
partisan warfare	and	Valley Forge
Saratoga	and	French Treaty of Alliance and Commerce
Elizabeth Drinker	and	Cherry Valley, New York

Essays

1. Assess the extent to which the American Revolution, on balance, was good or bad for <u>five</u> of the following groups: northern farmers, Virginia slave owners, slaves, Native Americans, Loyalists, urban artisans and shopkeepers, frontier women.

2. Assess how well Americans were able to fulfill their Revolutionary republican ideology in the war and the postwar era.

3. Show how the ideology of republicanism, which developed during the war, reflected the colonial experience with England prior to the war.

Identify and interpret: Quotation
(that is, state who, what, where, when, and
why significant)

I cannot say that I think you are very generous to the ladies; for, whilst you are proclaiming peace and goodwill to men, emancipating all nation, you insist upon retaining an absolute power over wives. But you must remember, that arbitrary power is like most other things which are very hard, very liable to be broken; and, notwithstanding all your wise laws and maxims, we have it in our power, not only to free ourselves, but to subdue our masters, and, without violence, throw both your natural and legal authority at our feet.

7

Consolidating the Revolution

(1) CHAPTER OUTLINE

Timothy Bloodworth of New Hanover County, North Carolina, rises from humble origins and gains a substantial position in his community and the respect of his neighbors. Although he becomes a delegate to the Confederation Congress in 1784, he soon loses confidence in the Articles of Confederation and supports the call for a special convention to meet in Philadelphia in 1787. When he views the constitution that emerges from that convention, however, he fears that the gains of the Revolution will be lost. He works tirelessly to defeat the new proposal. As a result of his efforts and the efforts of men like him, North Carolina only endorsed the new union when the Congress had forwarded a national bill of rights to the state for its approval.

Struggling with the Peacetime Agenda

> Demobilizing the Army
> Opening the West
> Wrestling with the National Debt
> Surviving in a Hostile World

Political Tumult in the States

> The Limits of Republican Experimentation
> Shay's Rebellion

Toward A New National Government

    The Rise of Federalism
    The Grand Convention
    Federalists Versus Anti-Federalists
    The Struggle for Ratification
    The Social Geography of Ratification

Conclusion: Completing the Revolution

(2) SIGNIFICANT THEMES AND HIGHLIGHTS

1. As the anecdote of Timothy Bloodworth suggests, this chapter explores the uncertain world facing Americans after the Revolutionary war had ended. Many feared the new government would not be able to assure settlement of the country's interior or pay off the massive war debt. The new nation was a weak newcomer in a world still dominated by powers like Great Britain.

2. The frantic pace of political experimentation on the state level moderated after 1783 as conservative arrangements replaced some of the radical ones passed only a few years earlier. As Shay's Rebellion suggested, however, many had not forgotten the cries for equal rights and popular consent that had been so powerfully expressed in 1776.

3. This chapter presents the political controversies marking the writing and ratification of the Constitution and explains the struggle for ratification of that document.

(3) LEARNING GOALS

Familiarity with Basic Knowledge

After reading this chapter, you should be able to:

1. Describe the terms of the land ordinances of 1785 and 1787 and the ideas behind the conquest theory.

2. Itemize the steps taken by Robert Morris to deal with the national debt.

3. Explain the causes and consequences of Shay's Rebellion.

4. Describe the reasons for dissatisfaction with the Articles of Confederation.

5. State the major compromises worked out at the Constitutional Convention and the major features of the original Constitution--its organizational format and the most significant allocations of power, rights, and responsibilities.

6. Outline the major arguments of Federalists and Anti-Federalists in the debates over ratification of the Constitution.

Practice with Historical Thinking Skills

After reading this chapter, you should be able to:

1. Explain the reasons for the success of the Federalists in writing and securing the ratification of the Constitution.

2. Analyze how the Constitution changed and strengthened the government that had existed under the Articles of Confederation.

3. Describe the different political and social perspectives of the Federalists and Anti-Federalists.

(4) IMPORTANT DATES TO KNOW

1784	Treaty of Fort Stanwix with Iroquois Spain closes Mississippi River to American navigation
1784-1786	Agrarian protest in several states
1785	Land Ordinance for Northwest Territory
1786	Annapolis convention calls for revision of Articles of Confederation
1786-1787	Shay's Rebellion
1787	Northwest Ordinance Constitutional Convention Convened
1788	Federalist Papers published by Hamilton, Jay, and Madison

Other Names to Know

Robert Morris   James Madison
Alexander Hamilton   John Jay

(5) GLOSSARY OF IMPORTANT TERMS

<u>relief ("stay") laws:</u> state laws desired by debtors and
    farmers in hard times that would suspend the collection
    of private debts and the foreclosure of farms for a
    specified period

<u>elastic clauses</u>: clauses in the Constitution, such as article
    1, section 8, granting Congress the power "to make all
    laws necessary and proper" for carrying out its other
    powers, which enabled the central government to expand
    its activities

(6) ENRICHMENT IDEAS

1. Find an Indian treaty for the Native Americans in
    your region and discover what it suggests about the
    attitudes and values of both the white and Native
    American treaty-makers.

2. The complete text of the United States Constitution
    is found in the appendix of <u>The American
    People</u>. Read and study the Constitution, breaking it
    down into its major parts, and identify the five or
    so most significant points to remember in each part.

3. Make a chart contrasting the major differences between
    the Declaration of Independence and the
    Constitution over their primary purposes, the
    quality and style of language, political ideology,
    assumptions about human nature and ends of
    government, and how to achieve political change.

(7) SAMPLE TEST AND EXAMINATION QUESTIONS

Multiple choice: Choose the best answer.

1. The Continental Congress
    a. successfully opened western lands after the Revolution.
    b. quelled Indian resistance to white western migration
    c. were unable to open the interior
    d. gave all western lands to speculators

2. Shay's Rebellion revealed that
    a. farmers wanted more gold coin in circulation
    b. authority under the Articles of Confederation was too weak
    c. the American Revolution had succeeded in shifting the balance of power from the rich to the poor
    d. the court system was responsive to the needs of the people

3. The Federalists believed all of the following except that
    a. the national government should be stronger
    b. there were "natural distinctions" between people
    c. there was a crisis threatening the nation's survival
    d. the states should assume more powers

4. During the postwar years, the Continental Congress treated Native Americans of the interior
    a. as if they were sovereign nations
    b. as if they were military foes
    c. no differently than they had in colonial times
    d. as if they were conquered peoples

5. The Virginia Plan differed most significantly from the New Jersey Plan by calling for
    a. a bicameral Congress and a whole new national government
    b. revision of the Articles of Confederation by letting Congress choose a president
    c. revision of the Articles by providing for equal representation in both houses of Congress
    d. the abolition of the executive branch

6. The Constitution clearly shows that the founding
   fathers
   a. wanted to abolish slavery
   b. were prepared to lay the groundwork for eventual
      equal rights between whites and blacks
   c. provided for the protection of slavery
   d. were willing to abolish only three-fifths of the
      slaves

7. That the Constitution shifted power from the states
   to the central government is made evident by giving
   Congress power
   a. to lay and collect taxes
   b. to regulate foreign and domestic commerce
   c. to pass all laws "necessary and proper" for
      carrying out other powers
   d. all of the above

8. According to the Constitution, Congress has all of
   the following powers except the power
   a. to declare war
   b. to borrow money
   c. to tax exports
   d. to lay and collect taxes

9. According to the Constitution, the executive branch
   has all of the following powers except that of
   a. declaring wars
   b. enforcing laws
   c. making judicial appointments
   d. commanding the army and navy

10. According to the Constitution, treaties, in order to
    become the law of the land, must be approved by
    a. a majority of the Senate
    b. two-thirds of the House
    c. two-thirds of the Senate
    d. three-fourths of both houses of Congress

11. Anti-Federalists believed that
    a. the Constitutional Convention was unfortunate
       but thoroughly legal
    b. separation of powers was enough to prevent the
       abuse of power in the new government
    c. republican liberty was best preserved by the
       balancing of factions
    d. republican liberty was best preserved in small,
       simple, homogeneous societies

74

12. Madison argued in <u>Federalist</u> <u>No. 10</u> that factions were
    a. less likely to destroy liberty in a large republic than in a small one
    b. more likely to destroy liberty in a large republic than in a small one
    c. undemocratic and therefore should be suppressed
    d. good for homogeneous states but unnecessary in a federal system

13. The ratification process revealed that Federalist strength was strongest
    a. in small interior farm regions
    b. in coastal cities and towns
    c. in the South except for Georgia
    d. among merchants but not working-class artisans and workers

True or False: Questions on the U.S. Constitution:

_T_ 1. The Constitution (plus laws and treaties) is the supreme law of the land.

_F_ 2. The Constitution created a Supreme Court and 13 district courts.

_T_ 3. Congress has the power to coin money.

_T_ 4. Congress may not tax exports.

_F_ 5. The president makes treaties with the approval of two-thirds of Congress.

_T_ 6. The president appoints ambassadors, judges, and other officials with the advice and consent of the Senate.

_F_ 7. To be a senator, one must be at least 35 years old.

_T_ 8. Treason consists of levying war against the United States or giving aid and comfort to the enemy.

_F_ 9. Slaves and indentured servants count as three-fifths of a person for purposes of representation.

_T_ 10. All bills for raising revenue must originate in the House of Representatives.

_T_ 11. New states may be admitted to the Union by Congress.

T 12. The United States may intervene against domestic violence within a state.

F 13. The president declares war with the approval of two-thirds of Congress.

F 14. The phrase "life, liberty, and the pursuit of happiness" from the Declaration of Independence, reappears in the Constitution.

F 15. The president shares with federal courts the power "to faithfully execute the laws."

T 16. Amendments may be proposed by either two-thirds of Congress or the states (in legislatures or conventions) and must be ratified by three-quarters of the states (in legislatures or conventions).

F 17. The First Amendment guarantees the rights of speech, press, petition, religion, and bearing of arms.

Essays

1. Show how the roots of the main provisions of the Constitution are in the colonial experience under English rule as well as in the Articles of Confederation period.

2. To what extent do you agree with Fisher Ames's question as to whether the rulers in a democracy may use physical force to maintain domestic order without turning public opinion against them? Discuss, drawing your evidence from the history of the United States in the 1780s.

Identify and Interpret: Quotation
(that is, state who, what, where, when, and why significant)

That this is a consolidated government is demonstrably clear; and the danger of such a government is, to my mind, very striking. I have the highest veneration for those gentlemen; but, sir, say, We, the people? My political curiosity, exclusive of my anxious solicitude for the public welfare, leads me to ask, Who authorized them to speak the language of We the people, instead of, We, the states? States are the characteristics and the soul of a confederation.

8

Creating a Nation

(1) Chapter Outline

David Brown, Revolutionary War veteran, seaman, and pamphleteer, increasingly attacked the central government under the new national constitution in the 1790s. He claimed it was a conspiracy of the rich to exploit farmers, artisans, and other common folk. His inflammatory charges aroused the ire of the federal judiciary, which convicted him of sedition and put him in prison. He was released only after the election of Thomas Jefferson in 1800.

Launching the National Republic

      Launching the New Government
      The People Divide
      The Whiskey Rebellion

The Republic in a Threatening World

      The Promise and Peril of the
      French Revolution
      Citizen Genet and the Democratic-Republican
      Societies
      Jay's Controversial Treaty

Federalists versus Jeffersonians

      The Election of 1796

War Crisis with France
Alien and Sedition Acts
Local Reverberations
The "Revolution of 1800"

Conclusion: Toward the Nineteenth Century

(2) SIGNIFICANT THEMES AND HIGHLIGHTS

1. As David Brown's story suggests, this chapter presents the turbulent political controversies surrounding launching of the new government in the 1790s.

2. The struggle to create a nation was marked by the formation of two political parties, Federalists and Democratic-Republicans, and by crises in the young nation's relationships with France and England during the presidential administrations of George Washington and John Adams.

3. Underlying the political controversies of the 1790s, as David Brown's life reveals, were class differences between rich and poor, regional differences between the urban Northeast and the interior West and South, and two conflicting ideological views over issues of power, political equality, and the proper role of central government in a republican society.

(3) LEARNING GOALS

Familiarity with Basic Knowledge

After reading this chapter, you should be able to:

1. Describe the Bill of Rights.

2. Outline Hamilton's view of the proper role of government, his financial plan, and the fate of each proposal.

3. State the major events of George Washington's administration, including the causes of the Whiskey Rebellion.

4. State how the French Revolution divided Americans and contributed to the development of party politics.

78

5. Describe the social composition, political principles, and activities of the Democratic-Republican societies.

6. Describe the major domestic and foreign crises of the administration of John Adams.

Practice in Historical Thinking Skills

After reading this chapter, you should be able to:

1. Discuss the disagreement over the role of government in the new nation.

2. Compare and contrast the differing ideological positions and visions of the Federalists and the Democratic-Republicans in the 1790s.

3. Decide whether the election of 1800 was, as Jefferson thought, "a revolution in the principles of our government."

(4) IMPORTANT DATES AND NAMES TO KNOW

1789	Inauguration of Washington as first president Outbreak of French Revolution
1790	Hamilton's "Reports on the Public Credit"
1791	Bill of Rights ratified Whiskey tax and national bank established Bank of the United States chartered
1793-1794	Outbreak of war in Europe Whiskey Rebellion in Pennsylvania
1794	Controversy over Citizen Genet's visit
1795	Jay's Treaty with England divides nation
1796	Washington's Farewell Address John Adams elected president
1797	XYZ affair in France
1798	Naturalization Act; Alien and Sedition Acts Trials of David Brown and Luther Baldwin Virginia and Kentucky resolutions

1800   Adams achieves "peace" with France
                Jefferson elected president by House of
                Representatives

Other Names to Know

James Madison   John Jay
Aaron Burr   Talleyrand
John Marshall

(5) GLOSSARY OF IMPORTANT TERMS

<u>federalism:</u> a form of government in which power is distrib-
    uted to and shared by different political levels, as
    between states and the central government

<u>federalists:</u> supporters of the ratification of the Consti-
    tution and the shift of power from local and state
    governments to the central government

<u>Federalists:</u> political party organized in the 1790s under
    Hamilton and John Adams dedicated to a strong central
    government, national power and economic growth, and rule
    by the wealthy elite

<u>Democratic-Republican societies:</u> popular associations in
    America that supported the ideals of revolutionary
    France and became the basis of the Jeffersonian Repub-
    lican party

(6) ENRICHMENT IDEAS

1. After examining the paintings in the RTP and opening
    for this chapter, look up and study other patriotic
    paintings of the Revolutionary era by John Barralot,
    John Trumbull, Gilbert Stuart, Charles Willson Peale,
    and others. What kind of mythology do they depict
    about the founding fathers? What kinds of
    mythologies exist today about American heroes? Are
    our heroes still political figures? If not, who are
    they? What does the choice of a nation's heroes
    suggest about that nation's values?

2. Make a chart contrasting the major ideas, political principles, and social composition of the two emerging political party traditions.

(7) SAMPLE TEST AND EXAMINATION QUESTIONS

Multiple choice: Choose the best answer.

1. The Bill of Rights was
   a. part of the original Constitution
   b. a leftover from the Articles of Confederation
   c. a means of creating support for the new government
   d. opposed because it pandered to the people

2. Hamilton believed that
   a. power belonged to the people
   b. most people had poor judgment
   c. the rich were no better than the poor
   d. none of the above

3. Alexander Hamilton
   a. was a financial and political conservative
   b. was forward-looking in his economic programs but politically conservative
   c. believed in free trade but opposed a protective tariff
   d. believed in distributing powers equally to both the executive and legislative branches of government

4. The primary objectives of Hamilton's financial program were
   a. to promote agricultural growth in the West
   b. to establish the country's credit with the French
   c. to promote commercial expansion overseas
   d. all of the above

5. Jefferson believed that
   a. the government should only have powers specifically designated by the Constitution
   b. Hamilton's programs represented a reasonable solution to the new nation's problems
   c. the yeoman farmer and the city artisan were the backbone of the republic
   d. Hamilton's proposal for the bank would hinder the development of commerce and manufacturing

81

6. The Whiskey Rebellion was fomented by
    a. Revolutionary War veterans still angry about
        taxation without representation
    b. western Federalists jealous of Hamilton's power
        over Washington
    c. resentful farmers whose livelihood was threatened
        by the tax on whiskey
    d. tavernkeepers

7. The French Revolution
    a. was a radical social revolution
    b. divided both Europeans and Americans
    c. offered Americans trading opportunities
    d. all of the above

8. The Democratic-Republican societies
    a. supported revolutionary France
    b. supported American neutrality in the European
        wars
    c. were led by common working people
    d. sought to remove both French and English
        influence from the United States

9. Jay's Treaty
    a. succeeded in removing the British from western
        fur-trading posts
    b. resolved almost none of America's grievances with
        England
    c. provided guarantees against the impressment of
        American seamen
    d. opened the West Indies to American shipping

10. John Adams and Thomas Jefferson
    a. had similar ideas on the role of the national
        government
    b. were contending for the leadership of the
        Federalist party
    c. had been enemies from the time of the Continental
        Congress
    d. had divergent ideas about the development of the
        new nation

11. The Alien and Sedition Acts
    a. nearly succeeded in squelching Jeffersonian
        criticism of Federalist policies
    b. were aimed at advocates of a strong navy
    c. were declared unconstitutional by the Supreme
        Court
    d. were attacked by Jefferson but defended in
        Madison's Virginia Resolutions

12. The "Revolution of 1800"
    a. was the occasion of the passage of the Bill of Rights
    b. revealed strong sectional divisions
    c. represented yet another Federalist victory
    d. was decided definitively in the electoral college

13. The Federalists
    a. had strong support in the South as well as in the North
    b. had a strong following among agriculturalists
    c. had mainly northern support
    d. were so weak no one supported the party

Essays

1. Compare and contrast the ideological positions and visions of the Federalists and the Jeffersonian Republicans in the 1790s.

2. Analyze and evaluate the reasons for the dominance of Federalist party principles in the 1790s.

3. Explain the reasons for the rise of political parties in the 1790s.

Identify and Interpret: Quotation
(that is, state who, what, where, when, and why significant)

"To conclude-Here's success to honest TOM PAINE:
May he live to enjoy what he does well explain.
The just Rights of Man we never forget
For they'll save Britain's friends from the
BOTTOMLESS PITT."

"Less respect to the consuming speculator, who wallows in luxury, than to the productive mechanic, who struggles with indigence."

9

Politics and Society in the Early Republic

(1) CHAPTER OUTLINE

Handsome Lake, a Seneca Indian, fashions a message of renewal and hope for his people. His revival draws from Native American traditions as well as from the values and ideas of white culture. The revitalization that Handsome Lake promotes is only one of the strategies Native American tribes pursue in the early decades of the nineteenth century.

Restoring Republican Liberty

The Jeffersonian Republicans Take Control
Cleansing the Government
The Judiciary and the Principle of Judicial Review
Dismantling the Federal War Program

Building an Agrarian Republic

The Jeffersonian Vision
The Windfall Louisiana Purchase
Exploring and Opening the Trans-Mississippi West

Indian-White Relations in the Early Republic

Land and Trade
Civilizing a "Savage" People
Strategies of Survival: The Cherokee

Patterns of Armed Resistance: The Shawnee
and the Creek

A Foreign Policy for the Agrarian Republic

Jeffersonian Principles
Struggling for Neutral Rights
The War of 1812
The United States and the Americas

Culture and Politics in Transition

The Tensions of Republican Culture
Politics in Transition
The Specter of Sectionalism
A New Style of Politics
Collapse of the Federalist-Jeffersonian Party

Conclusion: The Passing of an Era

(2) SIGNIFICANT THEMES AND HIGHLIGHTS

1. This chapter focuses on the first three decades of
   the nineteenth century, a period of intense political
   activity and westward expansion. The chapter
   emphasizes the attempts of the Jeffersonian
   Republicans to reshape national political life and to
   realize their vision of liberty in an agrarian
   republic.

2. As the anecdote of Handsome Lake suggests, the chapter continues the story of Indian-white relations.
   Between 1790 and 1820, tribal groups developed
   strategies of resistance and survival. Some tribes,
   like the Seneca whom Handsome Lake inspired,
   underwent cultural renewal. Others, like the
   Cherokee, adopted many of the ways of white society.
   Still others, like the Shawnee and Creek nations,
   chose armed resistance. At the same time, federal
   policies were developed, based on both humanitarian
   and territorial concerns, that would guide
   Indian-white relations for the rest of the
   nineteenth century.

3. In the field of foreign affairs, Jeffersonians
   attempted to fashion policies that would free the
   nation of entangling alliances with European powers,
   eliminate foreign troops from American soil, and
   protect American maritime interests. Although

foreign policy measures were in the short run unsuccessful, as the War of 1812 indicated, the United States soon stated its unique claim to the Western Hemisphere.

4. Efforts to create a distinctive American culture faltered because of disagreements over the value of the country's English heritage and because of the association of culture with social class.

(3) LEARNING GOALS OF THIS CHAPTER

Familiarity with Basic Knowledge

After reading this chapter, you should be able to:

1. Explain three measures Jefferson took to reshape and cleanse the federal government.

2. List the main functions of the federal government in the early nineteenth century.

3. Explain the reasons why Jefferson believed agricultural life was essential to political liberty.

4. Show how changing land acts affected settlement of the public domain.

5. Show the conflicting goals of federal Indian policy.

6. Outline the causes and significance of the War of 1812 and of the Monroe Doctrine.

Practice in Historical Thinking Skills

After reading this chapter, you should be able to:

1. Compare and contrast the survival strategies of the Cherokee, Shawnee, and Creek nations and evaluate how well you think their different strategies worked.

2. Discuss the validity of the American claim that the War of 1812 was the "second War of American Independence."

3. Explain the forces that weakened Jefferson's party.

(4) IMPORTANT DATES AND NAMES TO KNOW

1788	Treaty of Fort Harmar Knox's reports on Indian affairs
1794	Battle of Fallen Timbers
1795	Treaty of Greenville
1800	Capital moves to Washington Thomas Jefferson elected president Second Great Awakening begins
1801	Judiciary Act New Land Act
1802	Repeal of Judiciary Act
1803	Marbury v. Madison Louisiana Purchase
1803-1806	Lewis and Clark expedition
1803-1812	Napoleonic Wars resume British impress American sailors
1804	Jefferson reelected
1805-1806	Pike's explorations in the West
1806	Non-Importation Act
1807	Chesapeake incident Embargo Act
1808	James Madison elected president Cherokee legal code established
1809	Tecumseh's Confederacy formed Non-Intercourse Acts
1810	Macon's Bill No.2 American Fur Trade Company established
1811	Battle of Kithtippecanoe
1812	War of 1812 with England declared Annexation of western Florida Madison reelected
1813	Battle of Thames River

1814	Hartford Convention convenes Treaty of Ghent
1815	Battle of New Orleans United States establishes military posts in trans-Mississippi West
1816	James Monroe elected president Second Bank of the United States chartered
1819	Transcontinental Treaty with Spain Spain cedes East Florida to United States McCulloch v. Maryland
1820	Land Act Monroe reelected Missouri Compromise
1823	Monroe Doctrine proclaimed
1824	John Quincy Adams elected president
1827	Cherokees adopt written constitution

Other Names to Know

John Ross	Tecumseh
Elskwatawa	Robert Calhoun

(5) GLOSSARY OF IMPORTANT TERMS

full-blooded: term applied to Indians who had only Indian blood to distinguish them from mixed-blooded Indians

War Hawks: a group of Republican leaders, including Clay and Calhoun, who pressed for a warlike stance toward Great Britain and urged territorial expansion into Canada and Florida

(6) ENRICHMENT IDEAS

1. Do the imaginary map exercise described in the RTP for this chapter. Then turn to an actual outline map of the United States and trace the route of the Lewis and Clark expedition. Fill in the area acquired in

the Louisiana Purchase and trace the Transcontinental Treaty Line of 1819 (Adams-Onis). What conclusions do you draw about the relationship between exploration and expansion? Finally, add Florida, New Orleans, and other important battle sites of the War of 1812.

2. Develop a position paper supporting or rejecting war with Great Britain from the point of view of a member of Congress from the South, the West, and New England. What would be the differences between the positions and specific arguments of the three congressmen?

3. In the library, look at some of the volumes on American art. What materials are included from the period covered by this chapter? What has the author said about the art? What are your observations? Do they correspond to the views of American culture suggested in the concluding section of this chapter?

(7) SAMPLE TEST AND EXAMINATION QUESTIONS

Multiple choice: Choose the best answer.

1. Jeffersonians were initially concerned about all of the following except
   a. Federalist officeholders
   b. lame-duck appointments
   c. Adams's proposal for an elected judiciary
   d. the Judiciary Act

2. In the Marbury v. Madison decision, Chief Justice Marshall
   a. declared the Maryland law taxing the Second Bank of the United States unconstitutional
   b. declared that the bank was unconstitutional
   c. affirmed the principle of exclusive judicial review
   d. all of the above

3. During Jefferson's administration
   a. the federal government sponsored an active program of internal improvements
   b. the provisional army was completely dismantled
   c. farmers were rewarded for homesteading
   d. none of the above

4. Jefferson
   a. believed Malthus's warnings about the impact of a
      growing population on food supply
   b. had not read Malthus
   c. had read Malthus but thought his analysis was
      flawed
   d. believed that America's land base would allow the
      country to avoid the impact of population growth

5. Jefferson felt justified in buying the Louisiana
   Territory
   a. because the Constitution allowed the president to
      acquire new territories
   b. because he was sure the country approved of his
      action
   c. because his party pressed him to acquire it
   d. because Napoleon was offering if for less than
      Jefferson had been prepared to spend

6. The federal government between 1790 and 1820
   a. continued to acquire Native American lands
   b. wanted to protect Indians from unscrupulous
      exploitation
   c. adopted a new treaty strategy
   d. all of the above

7. The Embargo Act
   a. forbade American ships from sailing to foreign
      ports
   b. prohibited the importation of English goods
   c. declared impressment illegal
   d. threatened to invoke an embargo on France or
      England if the other did not cease its violations
      of American neutral rights on the high seas

8. The most eager calls for war with Great Britain came
   from
   a. the Federalists
   b. western and southern Republicans
   c. New England merchants
   d. southern planters

9. The Hartford Convention was
   a. a meeting with Native American tribal leaders
   b. a meeting of the young War Hawks
   c. a meeting of New Englanders considering secession
   d. a secession meeting in South Carolina

10. The Treaty of Ghent
    a. resolved outstanding American differences with
       Great Britain
    b. avoided most important areas of dispute

c. contained an agreement that the British would evacuate western forts
d. resolved boundary disputes in the Oregon Territory

11. The Monroe Doctrine
   a. was a policy developed by Americans with the aid of British diplomats
   b. was distinctly anti-European in tone
   c. led to immediate American involvement in Latin American affairs
   d. put fear into the hearts of European diplomats

12. The Second Great Awakening
   a. represented a rejection of older views of predestination
   b. was a revival led by New England clergy
   c. affected urban dwellers first and then spread into rural areas
   d. emphasized ritual rather than reason

13. Between 1812 and 1828
   a. the Federalist party collapsed
   b. the Jeffersonian Republicans collapsed
   c. the Anti-Federalist party collapsed
   d. both (a) and (b) happened

14. After 1812, the government did all of the following except
   a. charter the First Bank of the United States
   b. pass the first protective tariff
   c. sponsor internal improvements
   d. stimulate economic expansion

15. When Jefferson said, "This momentous question, like a firebell in the night . . . [has] awakened and filled me with terror," he was referring to
   a. the Monroe Doctrine
   b. the Kansas-Nebraska Act
   c. Stono's rebellion
   d. the Missouri Compromise

Essays

1. Write an essay on the following statement: "Once in power, the Jeffersonian Republicans retreated from many of the positions they had held as the opposition party." Show the extent to which you agree with the statement, and support your position with evidence.

2. Write an essay showing what you think was meant by the statement that the Jeffersonian Republicans "out-federalized the Federalists."

3. The War of 1812 was not merely a war against an external foe but stemmed from internal problems as well. Write an essay taking this statement as your starting point.

4. Evaluate the survival strategies of several Native American nations and compare them with the foreign policy strategies of the young United States. Which was more successful, and why do you think so?

Identify and Interpret: Quotation
(that is, state who, what, where, when, and why significant)

Let us, then, with courage and confidence pursue our own Federal and Republican principles, our attachment to union and representative government. Kindly separated by nature and a wide ocean from the exterminating havoc of one quarter of the globe; too high-minded to endure the degradations of the others; possessing a chosen country, with room enough for our descendants to the thousandth and thousandth generation; entertaining a due sense of our equal right to the use of our own faculties, to the acquisitions of our own industry, to honor and confidence from our fellow-citizens, resulting not from birth, but from our actions and their sense of them; enlightened by a benign religion, professed, indeed, and practiced in various forms...with all these blessings, what more is necessary to make us a happy and a prosperous people? Still one thing more, fellow-citizens -- a wise and frugal Government, which shall restrain men from injuring one another, shall leave them otherwise free to regulate their own pursuits of industry and improvement, and shall not take from the mouth of labor the bread it has earned. This is the sum of good government, and this is necessary to close the circle of our felicities.

92

Map question:

Locate the following on the accompanying map.

1. Louisiana Territory
2. Spanish East Florida
3. Missouri Compromise Line
4. disputed Oregon Territory
5. Battle of Kithtippecanoe
6. New Orleans
7. Transcontinental Treaty Line of 1819
8. areas inhabited by the Shawnee, Cherokee, and Creek nations
9. Gulf Coast areas added during War of 1812
10. Constitutional Convention

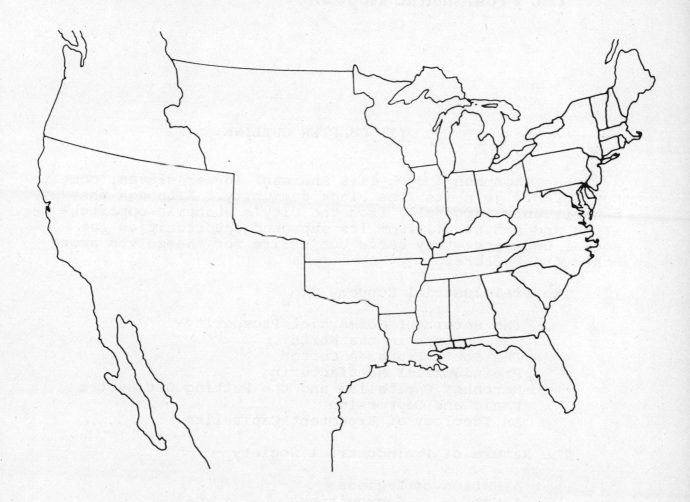

10

The Preindustrial Republic

(1) CHAPTER OUTLINE

Ben Thompson and Phyllis Sherman, former slaves, come to New York to join its free black community. Although they benefit only marginally from the city's economic opportunities and not at all from its supposed opportunities for social equality, they carve out a life for themselves among other free blacks.

The Preindustrial Economy

The Return of Commercial Prosperity
Agriculture in the North
The South Embraces Cotton
Preindustrial Manufacturing
Merchant Capitalism and the Putting Out System
Panic and Depression
An Ideology of Expectant Capitalism

The Nature of Preindustrial Society

A Nation of Regions
A Nation of Communities
Lives of Intimacy and Quietness
Lives of Difficulty and Trial
Birth, Death, and Disease
Patterns of Wealth and Poverty

Perfecting Republican Society

    The Youthfulness of America
    The Meaning of Social Equality
    The Doctrine of Individualism
    The Second Great Awakening and Social Reform
    Alleviating Poverty and Distress
    Educating the Republic's Children
    Women in Republican Society
    The Limits of Reform: Race and Slavery

Conclusion: Between Two Worlds

(2) SIGNIFICANT THEMES AND HIGHLIGHTS

1. This chapter surveys American life between 1790 and
    1820 and characterizes the period as one poised
    between old ways of life and new ones. It shows the
    continuities with the past--the dependence on
    overseas trade, the traditional rhythms of
    agricultural life, and the dominance of small-scale
    production, along with signs of change--commercial
    expansion, the rise of merchant capitalism, the birth
    of the cotton kingdom and the early textile industry,
    and changing modes of transportation.

2. The description of the local and personal character
    of preindustrial life and society includes regional
    differences in class systems and the troubling growth
    of poverty. Americans led lives that were "intimate
    and quiet" as well as rigorous and difficult.

3. The chapter explains the ideological underpinnings
    for changing attitudes toward economic growth and
    social equality as well as the ambivalent ways in
    which Americans attacked their social problems in the
    republican experiment.

Familiarity with Basic Knowledge

After reading this chapter, you should be able to:

1. List three reasons for the prosperity of the 1790s.

2. Explain why America's economic status can be described as neocolonial.

3. Show three changes in northern agriculture in the early nineteenth century and give four reasons for its limited productivity.

4. Explain the impact of the cotton gin on southern agriculture and show how cotton reinforced the institution of slavery.

5. Name three groups of Americans who were conspicuous among the nation's poor.

6. Explain why Americans were increasingly interested in reform.

Practice in Historical Thinking Skills

After reading this chapter, you should be able to:

1. Explain why Americans embraced capitalism in the early nineteenth century.

2. Describe the most striking aspects of early nineteenth-century communities and analyze the ways in which they were changing.

3. Explain the arguments that could be made in 1815 both to support the institution of slavery and to argue for its dissolution.

(4) IMPORTANT DATES AND NAMES TO KNOW

1776   Adam Smith's Wealth of Nations published

1790   First textile mill established in Pawtucket, Rhode Island

1791-1793   Black rebellion in Haiti

| 1793 | Eli Whitney invents the cotton gin |
| | Europe embroiled in war |

| 1794 | First Afro-American churches founded |

1790s	Turnpike construction in Northeast
	Yellow fever epidemics in cities
	Female academies founded
	Cotton production booms in South
	Beginning of Second Great Awakening

| 1800 | Aborted slave rebellion in Virginia |
| 1801 | Revival at Cane Ridge, Kentucky |

1807	Robert Fulton launches first steamboat
	Cast-iron plow patented
	Jefferson declares trade embargo
	U.S. slave trade ends

| 1809 | Embargo lifted |

| 1811 | Successful trip of steamboat from Ohio River to New Orleans |

| 1812 | War with Great Britain declared |

| 1816 | American Colonization Society formed |
| | Second U.S. Bank chartered |

| 1819 | Panic of 1819 |

Other Names to Know

Benjamin Rush   Robert Fulton

(5) GLOSSARY OF IMPORTANT TERMS

merchant capitalism: the stage of development during which
    merchants helped direct economic growth by investing
    surplus capital into domestic enterprises like manu-
    facturing

(6) ENRICHMENT IDEAS

1. Using the data on Ohio from the census returns of
    1820 in the RTP for this chapter, construct as full a
    picture as you can of family and household life in
    the early nineteenth century. What would these (or
    similar) counties look like today? How have family
    and household structures changed in the more than 165
    years since 1820, and how do you account for these
    changes?

2. There are several living-history farms and museum
    villages that seek to capture daily life in the
    period covered by this chapter. If you are located
    near Sturbridge Village in Massachusetts, Turkey Run
    Farm Park in Virginia, or another early nineteenth-
    century restored village make sure you visit them.
    What continuities do you see with life in the past?
    What signs of change? How accurately does the site
    interpretation convey the picture of life described
    in this chapter? If you were in charge of revising
    the interpretive program, what changes might you
    suggest?

3. Imagine yourself as either Ben Thompson or Phyllis
    Sherman, the two free blacks featured in the
    anecdote. How might they compare their life in New
    York with the lives they had led in Maryland and
    Connecticut? Make a list of the benefits and
    disadvantages of living in New York for free blacks.

4. Think of what you might write in a daily journal if
    you lived in a northern agricultural community, on a
    cotton plantation, in a port city, or on the
    frontier. What kinds of activities might you
    mention? In what ways would your life be one of
    "intimacy and quietness"? What might be your worries
    and concerns?

5. Historic houses dating from this period are to be
    found in many parts of the country. A visit to a
    house museum or a walking tour of older sections of
    an eastern city will reveal much about living
    standards, class structure, convenience, and comfort.

(7) SAMPLE TEST AND EXAMINATION QUESTIONS

Multiple choice: Choose the best answer.

1. In 1800, what was the approximate percentage of the
    American labor force engaged in agriculture?
    a. 37 percent
    b. 55 percent
    c. 75 percent
    d. 83 percent

2. In the early nineteenth century, northern farmers
    produced goods
    a. only for themselves and their families
    b. mostly for national markets
    c. mostly for international markets
    d. for themselves with a small surplus for sale

3. By 1820, more than half the country's export trade
    was of
    a. wheat
    b. whiskey
    c. cotton
    d. cloth

4. American merchants began to invest in manufacturing
    because
    a. European wars reduced the profits to be made from
        overseas trade
    b. they realized that American-made products were
        superior to English ones
    c. the government gave them tax breaks
    d. Great Britain captured the carrying trade

5. In Lynn, the shoemaking trade was
    a. dominated by independent master craftsmen
    b. dispersed in home industries
    c. a seasonal activity carried on by farming
        families
    d. controlled by merchant capitalists

6. In the South,
    a. there were few class differences between whites
    b. there was an increasing gap between slave owners
        and other whites
    c. most whites owned slaves
    d. there was more opportunity to rise than in the
        North

7. Most city dwellers had
   a. a varied diet because they had small gardens
   b. a varied diet because city markets provided them with fresh produce
   c. limited diets
   d. refrigerators

8. Drinking rates were high among
   a. young working-class whites
   b. immigrants
   c. westerners
   d. all of the above

9. In 1800, the primary means of information linking American communities was
   a. newspapers and mail
   b. the pony express
   c. turnpike travel
   d. the telegraph

10. In 1800, the top 10 percent of property holders controlled about what percentage of the nation's wealth?
    a. 10 percent
    b. 30 percent
    c. 40 percent
    d. 70 percent

11. American values emphasized all of the following except
    a. youthfulness
    b. social equality
    c. social security
    d. individualism

12. During the early nineteenth century, women achieved modest gains in status in the areas of
    a. education and political rights
    b. property and political rights
    c. education and divorce
    d. higher education and legal rights

13. The education of girls was
    a. similar to that of boys
    b. geared toward preparing them to become wives and mothers
    c. was focused on training them in the accomplishments of gentility
    d. thought unnecessary

14. In the 50 years after the Revolution, vital
    communities of free blacks emerged in
    a. northern port cities
    b. the black belt of the rural South
    c. southern cities away from the black belt
    d. none of the above

Essays

1. Items 1-3 in the section Practice In Historical
    Thinking Skills under "Learning Goals" can be used to
    construct essay questions.

2. The 1790s was a decade that foreshadowed the regional
    splits that would lead to the Civil War. Discuss,
    citing specific evidence.

3. The American emphasis on social equality did not lead
    to sameness but rather to social, economic, and
    racial diversity. Discuss.

4. Did Americans in the early nineteenth century lead
    lives more of "intimacy and quietness" or of
    "difficulty and trial"? Explain your answer with
    specific examples drawn from American history between
    1790 and 1820.

PART THREE

AN EXPANDING PEOPLE
1820–1877

11

Currents of Change in the Northeast and the Old Northwest

(1) CHAPTER OUTLINE

Mary Paul works in the Lowell mills as a young girl of 15 and finds her situation exhilarating. Over the next few years, however, she discovers some of the disadvantages of mill work. Like many Americans, she finds economic change brings both new opportunities and new uncertainties.

Economic Growth

> Components of Growth
> Immigration
> Transportation: The Critical Factor
> Capital Investment
> The Role of Government
> The Innovative Mentality
> Ambivalence Toward Change
> The Advance of Industrialization

The Manufacturing World

> The Impact of Industrialization
> A New England Textile Town
> Working and Living in a Mill Town
> Female Responses to Work
> The Changing Character of the Work Force
> Factories on the Frontier

The Urban World

    The Process of Urbanization
    Class Structure in the Cities
    The Urban Working Class
    Middle-Class Life and Ideals
    Mounting Urban Tensions
    The Black Underclass

Rural Communities

    Farming in the East
    Frontier Families
    Opportunities in the Old Northwest

Conclusion: The Character of Progress

(2) SIGNIFICANT THEMES AND HIGHLIGHTS

1. This chapter, as Mary Paul's experience suggests, concentrates on the economic and social transformations in the Northeast and the Midwest between 1820 and 1860. The chapter discusses the factors contributing to economic growth, particularly the importance of changes in transportation, and explores industrialization as a new means of production and as a source of social change. The chapter shows that the process of industrialization was uneven, as old and new ways of production existed side by side.

2. Five types of communities (Lowell; Philadelphia; Cincinnati; Hampshire County, Massachusetts; and the Indiana frontier) are discussed to show how each participated in economic growth. The ways in which different classes, ethnic groups, and races responded to new conditions and shared or failed to share in the benefits of growth are highlighted.

3. The persistence of Revolutionary ideology is evident in working-class critiques of the new industrial world, while new middle-class ideals emerged as a response to changing economic and social conditions.

4. Samuel Breck and Joseph Sill, both of Philadelphia, are introduced as examples of upper- and middle-class urban dwellers. Several mill girls (Mary Paul and Sally Rice) appear at various points in the chapter. The Skinners give an idea of life on the Indiana frontier.

(3) LEARNING GOALS

Familiarity with Basic Knowledge

After reading this chapter, you should be able to:

1. List several factors contributing to economic growth and explain how changes in transportation were of critical importance.

2. Define the term _industrialization_ and identify the parts of the United States where industrialization took hold between 1830 and 1860.

3. Define the _cult of domesticity_ and explain the reasons for its development and describe new views of childhood.

4. Describe urban class structure and compare it to rural class structure.

5. Explain the process of establishing a family farm on the midwestern frontier.

6. Discuss the contribution of nontangible factors to economic growth.

Practice in Historical Thinking Skills

After reading this chapter, you should be able to:

1. Show how Cincinnati illustrates the uneven process of industrialization and the emergence of new types of work and new workers and contrast the situation in Cincinnati with the Lowell system.

2. Analyze the ways in which both male and female workers used Revolutionary ideology as a means of criticizing the new work order.

3. Summarize the ways in which economic and social changes affected people's lives both by increasing opportunities and benefits and by separating people from one another.

(4) IMPORTANT DATES AND NAMES TO KNOW

1805   Palmer v. Mulligan

1815   Waltham textile mills established

1817-1850   Construction of canals in the Northeast

1819   Dartmouth College v. Woodward

1820   Lowell founded by Boston Associates
                Land Act of 1820
                The term woman's sphere becomes current

1825   Completion of Erie Canal

1825-1856   Construction of canals linking Ohio and Mississippi
                rivers with the Great Lakes

1828   Baltimore and Ohio Railroad begins operation

1830   Preemption Act

1830s   Boom in the Old Northwest
                Increasing discrimination against free blacks
                Public education movement spreads

1833   Philadelphia establishes small police force

1834   Philadelphia race riot
                Lowell work stoppage

1837   Thomas Mann becomes secretary of Massachusetts Board
                of Education

1837-1844   Financial panic and depression

1840   Agitation for ten-hour day

1841   Distribution-Preemption Act

1840s-1850s   Rising tide of immigration

Other Names to Know

Sarah Hale   Catherine Beecher
Prudence Crandall

(5) GLOSSARY OF IMPORTANT TERMS

economic growth: an increase in output, usually involving not only expansion but changes in the methods of production

Waltham System: The system of textile production in which all stages of the manufacturing process were brought together

cult of domesticity: set of beliefs insisting that women had different characteristics than men, which made them best suited for the private sphere of home and family

entrepreneur: one who takes the risks of starting new ventures or one who owns or manages one or more businesses

industrial mode of production: the reorganization of production, breaking the process into a series of separate steps done by individual workers or machines

outwork: work done at home or in small shops; workers were usually paid by the piece

(6) ENRICHMENT IDEAS

1. Using the RTP as your guide, explore some volumes of early nineteenth-century paintings. What can you discover about the nature of daily life, attitudes, and values from your study?

2. Think how you might write an article for a Cincinnati newspaper evaluating some of the changes in work in the antebellum period if you were the owner of a furniture factory, a widow taking in piecework, or a former cabinetmaker now working in the factory.

3. Write a diary entry for one day in the life of a Lowell mill girl in the 1830s. Give a clear sense of your daily schedule as well as your response to your job and free time. How would your entry differ if you were an Irish girl in the 1850s?

4. If you live in the Midwest, visit the Conner Prairie Settlement near Indianapolis. This living-history museum, which uses first-person interpreters as villagers, conveys a realistic picture of daily life

106

on the frontier in the 1830s. Other living museums can suggest the ways in which rural American life changed in the period before the Civil War.

5. If you live in or near a northeastern or Middle Atlantic city, plan a walking tour to the part of the city constructed during the period covered by this chapter. What kinds of buildings date from that era? What were they used for? Are there any examples of housing? What class of persons may have lived in these houses? Are there any remaining evidences of working-class neighborhoods? Visit an early mill complex. What can it tell you about the industrial process, the nature of work, and the reality of life in a mill community?

(7) SAMPLE TEST AND EXAMINATION QUESTIONS

Multiple choice: Choose the best answer.

1. The Lowell work force was typically made up of
   a. married women
   b. married men
   c. single women in their thirties and forties
   d. single women between 15 and 29

2. Lowell mill owners constructed boardinghouses for their workers because
   a. they believed workers needed comfortable housing
   b. they wanted to attract a respectable work force
   c. they believed privacy was essential after a long day of toil
   d. they were copying European models

3. In 1840, about what percentage of all Americans lived in cities?
   a. 2 percent
   b. 10 percent
   c. 25 percent
   d. 50 percent

4. Population growth in the early decades of the nineteenth century occurred because of
   a. the increasing size of families
   b. a dramatic drop in death rates
   c. an increase in foreign immigration, mainly from Ireland and Germany
   d. an increase in immigrants from eastern and southern Europe

5. State governments
    a. rarely gave economic entrepreneurs special
        advantages
    b. levied heavy taxes on business profits
    c. favored farmers
    d. gave loans for internal improvements

6. The courts
    a. were slow to recognize new attitudes toward
        property
    b. reinforced the notion that business contracts
        were binding
    c. were lenient toward debtors
    d. none of the above

7. Early textile mills clustered around waterways in
    a. the South
    b. New England
    c. the Middle Atlantic states
    d. in New England and the Middle Atlantic states

8. The Erie Canal connected
    a. the Great Lakes with New York City
    b. the Great Lakes with the Mississippi River
    c. Lake Erie with Lake Ontario
    d. all of the above

9. The composition of the Lowell work force changed
    because
    a. women got married and therefore did not need the
        money
    b. women found they could earn more in other jobs
    c. mill owners preferred to hire Irish immigrants,
        who worked for less
    d. unions successfully organized the mills

10. The cult of domesticity suggested
    a. that while men and women were substantially
        similar, women belonged in the private sphere
    b. that women should make vital economic
        contributions to their families
    c. that women's innate differences from men made
        them suitable only for the private sphere
    d. that women belonged in the public sphere

11. Most Cincinnati workers labored
    a. alone
    b. in small and medium-size shops
    c. in large factories
    d. alongside slaves

12. City services in Philadelphia were provided for
    a. all citizens
    b. all white citizens
    c. all but the Irish
    d. those who could pay for them

13. Between 1830 and 1860,
    a. the gap between the urban rich and the poor
       narrowed
    b. many of the poor entered the middle class
    c. the gap between rich and poor widened
    d. little changed

14. Rural Americans in the Northeast
    a. had little contact with new economic trends
    b. were born, raised, and died in the same
       communities
    c. began to change traditional patterns as they came
       into contact with the industrial world
    d. enjoyed rough social and economic equality

15. Many Americans believed that free public education
    was important because
    a. they wanted their children to be independent
       thinkers
    b. it inculcated proper work habits
    c. it promoted social change
    d. it was a good way to keep children off the street

16. Horace Mann was
    a. an educational reformer
    b. an early manufacturer
    c. an inventor
    d. a resident of Philadelphia

17. Philadelphia had
    a. few blacks compared to other northern cities
    b. no blacks
    c. more blacks than other northern cities
    d. a socially homogeneous black community

    Identify and show a relationship between each of the
following pairs.

falling birth rates	and	new views of childhood
Lowell mills	and	Philadelphia
Irish immigration	and	frontier farming
Philadelphia race riot	and	Lowell work stop-page of 1834
cult of domesticity	and	Dartmouth v. Woodward

Essays

1. Items 1-3 under <u>Practice in Historical Thinking Skills</u> in "Learning Goals" suggest topics for practice in essay writing.

2. The life of "intimacy and quietness" (see Chapter 10) was disintegrating in the decades between 1830 and 1860 and was replaced by a life of separateness and clamor. Discuss this statement with appropriate supporting evidence.

Identify and Interpret: Quotation
(that is, state who, what, where, when, and why significant)

Rules and Regulations to be attended to and followed by the Young Persons who come to Board in this House:

<u>Rule first:</u> Each one to enter the house without unnecessary noise or confusion, and hang up their bonnet, shawl, coat, etc., in the entry.

<u>Rule second:</u> Each one to have their place at the table during meals, the two which have worked the greatest length of time in the Factory to sit on each side of the head of the table, so that all new hands will of course take their seats lower down, according to the length of time they have been here.

<u>Rule third:</u> It is expected that order and good manners will be preserved at table during meals--and at all other times either upstairs or down.

<u>Rule fourth:</u> There is no unnecessary dirt to be brought into the house by the Boarders, such as apple cores or peels, or nut shells, etc.

<u>Rule fifth:</u> Each boarder is to take her turn in making the bed and sweeping the chamber in which she sleeps. . . .

<u>Rule eighth:</u> The doors will be closed at ten o'clock at night, winter and summer, at which time each boarder will be expected to retire to bed.

<u>Rule ninth:</u> Sunday being appointed by our Creator as a Day of Rest and Religious Exercises, it is expected that all boarders will have sufficient discretion as to pay suitable attention to the day, and. . . they will keep within doors and improve their time in reading, writing, and in other valuable and harmless employment.

12

Slavery and the Old South

(1) CHAPTER OUTLINE

Frederick Douglass learns from his masters about complex, intricate chains that bind slaves and masters to each other. He also learns that education is the way to freedom.

Building the Cotton Kingdom

> Economic Expansion
> White and Black Migrations
> The Dependence on Slavery
> Slavery and Class in the South
> The Nonslaveholding South

Morning: Master in the Big House

> The Burdens of Slaveholding
> Justifying Slavery

Noon: Slaves in House and Fields

> Daily Toil
> Slave Health
> Slave Law and the Family

Night: Slaves in Their Quarters

       Black Christianity
       The Power of Song
       The Enduring Family

Resistance and Freedom

       Forms of Black Protest
       Slave Revolts
       Free Blacks: Becoming One's Own Master

Conclusion: Douglass's Dream of Freedom

(2) SIGNIFICANT THEMES AND HIGHLIGHTS

1. The tremendous growth of agriculture in the Old South was dependent on cotton and slavery. But contrary to myth, the South was an area of great diversity, regionally, socially, and in terms of class and slave ownership. These differences bred tensions among whites as well as between masters and slaves.

2. Although slavery was a labor system, the chapter emphasizes the daily life and complex, entangled relationships of white masters and black slaves and points out the difficulties of generalizing about their relationships. The experiences of the family of rice planter Robert Allston suggests some of the dimensions of white slaveholders' lives, while the youth of Frederick Douglass illuminates the lives of black slaves.

3. A unique structure in this chapter discusses slavery in three sections: morning in the Big House, which focuses on white masters, noon in the fields, which looks at daily work and other hardships of the slaves; and nighttime in the quarters, which describes a slave culture and community centered around religion, music, the family, and other adaptive survivals from African culture.

4. Racism was not confined to the South but existed throughout American society. Racism as well as slavery limited black freedom. To a much lesser extent, southern slaveholders also suffered limitations on their freedom from the burdens of the slave system.

112

(3) LEARNING GOALS

Familiarity with Basic Knowledge

After reading this chapter, you should be able to:

1. Distinguish several geographic regions and describe the socioeconomic class variations of slaveholding patterns in the Old South.

2. Describe the burdens of slavery from the perspective of the slaveholders and explain five ways in which they justified slavery.

3. Describe a typical day on the plantation for slave men and women, both in the house and in the fields.

4. Explain the nature of black family life and culture in the slave quarters, including how religion, music, and folklore gave the slaves a sense of identity and self-esteem.

5. List five ways in which the slaves protested and resisted their situation.

Practice in Historical Thinking Skills

After reading this chapter, you should be able to:

1. Develop arguments for and against slavery from the perspective of southern slaveholders, nonslaveholding southerners, northern whites, slaves, and freed blacks.

2. Discuss and evaluate the question of who was "free" in southern antebellum society.

3. Identify the author's interpretation of slavery and other possible interpretations.

(4) IMPORTANT DATES AND NAMES TO KNOW

1787	Constitution adopted with proslavery provisions
1793	Eli Whitney invents cotton gin
1800	Gabriel Prosser conspiracy in Virginia
1807	External slave trade prohibited by Congress

1820	South becomes world's largest cotton producer
1822	Denmark Vesey's conspiracy in Charleston
1830s	Southern justification of slavery changes from a necessary evil to a positive good Character of slave system changes Southern laws regulating treatment and manumission of slaves change
1831	Nat Turner's slave revolt in Virginia
1845	Narrative of the Life of Frederick Douglass
1850s	Cotton boom
1851	Indiana State constitution excludes free blacks
1860	Cotton production and prices peak

Other Names to Know

George Fitzhugh   John Flintoff
Newton Knight   Robert and Adele Allston
Sophia and Hugh Auld

(5) GLOSSARY OF KEY TERMS

manumission: the freeing of slaves by individual owners

culture: the values and way of life of a group of people that
    gives the group a unifying identity

polygenesis: the belief that blacks were a separately created
    race and hence inherently inferior

Herrenvolk democracy: the theory in the antebellum South that
    although there were economic inequalities among whites,
    all whites still shared an equality in their superiority
    to all blacks, a theory that enabled the southern
    planter elite to minimize class antagonisms among whites

(6) ENRICHMENT IDEAS

1. Find more folktales and stories told by slaves and analyze what they reveal about slave culture. See Harold Courlander, A Treasury of Afro-American Folklore (1976) or J. Mason Brewer, American Negro Folklore (1968).

2. Listen to some slave spirituals and work songs and analyze them. What do they reveal about the slave experience and about attitudes toward religion? Notice the double meanings.

3. Are there any historical sites in your area related to slavery--for example, plantations, stations on the underground railroad, or slave markets? Do restored plantations give a balanced view of life on the old plantation, the slave quarters as well as the Big House?

4. Consider the heritage of slavery in modern society. To what extent does it still affect our lives and how?

5. Are blacks and whites more or less "free" today than they were during slavery? Are they more or less entangled with each other?

(7) SAMPLE TEST AND EXAMINATION QUESTIONS

Multiple choice: Choose the best answer.

1. Most southern families had
    a. fewer than ten slaves
    b. over ten slaves
    c. no slaves
    d. fewer than five slaves

2. By the 1850s, the largest number of slaves was found in
    a. Texas and Louisiana
    b. the Upper South of Virginia and Kentucky
    c. cities
    d. the black belt stretching from South Carolina across Georgia, Alabama, and Mississippi

3. What percentage of southern white families were slaveholders?
   a. 25 percent
   b. 50 percent
   c. 75 percent
   d. 90 percent

4. The most valuable export crop in the South was
   a. cotton
   b. corn
   c. rice
   d. tobacco

5. The southern economic endeavors with the greatest economic value were
   a. rice and hemp
   b. corn and hogs
   c. cotton and sugarcane
   d. shipbuilding and textiles

6. The typical southern slaveholding family had
   a. fewer than 10 slaves
   b. between 10 and 20 slaves
   c. about 20 slaves
   d. over 50 slaves

7. According to the author of Chapter 12, the worst feature of slavery was
   a. the denial of freedom
   b. whippings
   c. the break up of families
   d. vitamin deficiency and illness

8. The sociological justification of slavery based its argument primarily on
   a. the Bible
   b. the Constitution
   c. scientific assumptions
   d. history

9. After 1831, slaves were
   a. more easily given their freedom but treated more harshly
   b. treated less harshly but denied their freedom
   c. feared less than before
   d. given the right to vote

10. Which of the following statements is not true about slave women?
   a. they had networks for mutual support
   b. they were encouraged to have many children

116

c. they had no choice in their marriage partners
d. they sometimes resisted forcible sexual encounters by whites

11. African forms of religious expression
    a. gradually died out in the New World
    b. were too sinful to survive in civilized society
    c. survived in adapted form in the New World
    d. survived in the West Indies but not in the United States

12. The slave family
    a. was destroyed by the slave trade
    b. played a key role in achieving black self-esteem
    c. imitated the family patterns of whites
    d. transmitted black family patterns to whites

13. By the 1850s, the largest number of free blacks was in
    a. the North
    b. the Upper South
    c. the Lower South
    d. Canada

14. We know about the cultural life of slaves in the quarters at night because of
    a. overseers' reports
    b. slave narratives
    c. congressional investigating committees
    d. the diaries of northern visitors

15. Slave culture was expressed most clearly in
    a. songs sung in the fields during the day
    b. Robert Allston's prayer house
    c. religious meetings at night
    d. the incidence of runaways

    Identify and show a relationship between each of the following pairs.

    James Hammond   and   Newton Knight
    Frederick Douglass   and   Sophia Auld
    yeomen farmers   and   poor whites
    visible   and   invisible black
                                    religious institutions
    day-to-day resistance   and   Nat Turner's revolt

117

Essays

1. Describe four class levels of southern white society, and show how each might have defended or justified slavery as necessary or good for its self-interest. Which would have defended slavery most vigorously and why do you think so?

2. Compare and contrast some of the typical events in the daily life of a house slave and a field slave. Which would you have preferred to be and why?

3. Compare and contrast the attitudes of white southerners and white northerners toward blacks. How do you explain whatever differences seem to exist?

4. Describe four or five manifestations of slave culture. Be as specific as you can about sources and modes of expression. Which do you think best expressed authentic slave culture and why?

5. Present an interpretation of slavery from the point of view of three different historians. One sees slavery from the perspective of southern slaveholders, one from the viewpoint of northern white abolitionists, and one from the perspective of the slaves themselves. What would be the major differences?

13

Shaping America in The Antebellum Age

(1) CHAPTER OUTLINE

Emily and Marius Robinson are separated shortly after their marriage because of their ardent commitment to abolish slavery and to educate free blacks. Despite suffering many hardships of separation, sickness, and mob attack, they persist for a time in an effort to shape and reform American society.

The Political Response to Change

    Changing Political Culture
    Jackson's Path to the White House
    Old Hickory's Vigorous Presidency
    Jackson's Bank War and "Van Ruin's" Depression
    The Second American Party System

Religious Revival and Reform

    Finney and the Second Great Awakening
    Reform and Politics
    The Transcendentalists

Utopian Communitarianism

    Oneida and the Shakers
    Other Utopias
    Millerites and Mormons

Reforming Society

    Temperance
    Health and Sexuality
    Humanizing the Asylum
    Working-Class Reform

Abolitionism and Women's Rights

    Tensions Within Antislavery
    Flood Tide of Abolitionism
    Women's Rights

Conclusion: Perfecting America

(2) SIGNIFICANT THEMES AND HIGHLIGHTS

1. The social and economic changes of the 1830s were both promising and unsettling. This chapter explores the question of how people (both ordinary and prominent) sought to maintain some sense of control over their lives in the 1830s and 1840s. Some, like the Robinsons, poured their energies into reform. Others turned to politics, religion, and new communal life styles in order to shape their changing world.

2. Throughout the chapter social, political, cultural, and economic phenomena are interrelated and seen as a whole. The chapter merges two major events-- democratic Jacksonian politics and the many forms of perfectionist social reform. They began from distinctly different points of view but in fact shared more in common than has usually been recognized.

3. The explanation of politics in the age of Jackson looks at the social and ethnocultural basis of politics, while the analysis of revivalism, religion, and utopian communitarianism stresses the socioeconomic basis of these cultural phenomena.

4. The timeless dilemmas and problems of reformers, especially of temperance, abolitionist, and feminist reformers, is a sub-theme running through the chapter.

(3) LEARNING GOALS

Familiarity with Basic Knowledge

After reading this chapter, you should be able to:

1. Describe three ways in which political culture changed between the early 1820s and 1840.

2. Explain the course of events of the three major issues in Jackson's presidency--the tariff, the war against the bank, and Indian removal.

3. List and explain the leaders, principles, programs, and sources of support of the two major parties, Democrats and Whigs.

4. List several evils that Americans wanted to reform in the 1830s and 1840s and the major influences that contributed to the reform impulse.

5. Describe some of the purposes, patterns, and problems that most utopian communities shared.

6. Describe the major goals, tactics, and problems in the antebellum reform movements for temperance, abolitionism, and women's rights.

Practice in Historical Thinking Skills

After reading this chapter, you should be able to:

1. Analyze how Jacksonian politicians and social reformers both opposed one another and had much in common.

2. Explain the development of the second American party system, showing how it evolved from and differed from the first party system.

3. To understand and explain why people turn to politics, or to religion and revivalism, or to utopian communitarianism, or to specific issue reforms in order to shape their world; and then to explain how well these seemed to work.

(4) IMPORTANT DATES AND NAMES TO KNOW

1824   New Harmony established
John Quincy Adams elected president

1826   American Temperance Society founded

1828   Calhoun publishes Exposition and Protest
Andrew Jackson elected president
Tariff of Abominations

1828-1832   Rise of workingmen's parties

1829   David Walker's Appeal

1830   Webster-Hayne debate and Jackson-Calhoun toast
The Book of Mormon published by Joseph Smith
Indian Removal Act

1831   Garrison begins publishing The Liberator

1832   Nullification crisis
Calhoun resigns as vice-president
Bank War and Jackson's veto
Jackson reelected
Worcester v. Georgia

1833   Force Bill and Compromise tariff
Removal of deposits from U.S. Bank
   to state banks begun
American Anti-Slavery Society established

1834   New York Female Moral Reform Society founded
National Trades Union founded
Whig party established

1835-1836   Increasing incidents of mob violence

1836   Gag rule
Specie circular
Martin Van Buren (D) elected president

1837   Financial panic and depression begin
Sarah Grimke's, Letters on the Equality of the Sexe
Emerson's "American Scholar" address

1837-1838   Cherokee "Trail of Tears"

1840   William Henry Harrison elected president
American Anti-Slavery Society splits
World Anti-Slavery Convention

1840-1841	Transcendentalists found Hopedale and Brook Farm
1843	Dorothea Dix's report on treatment of the insane Henry Highland Garnet's call for slave rebellion
1844	Joseph Smith murdered in Nauvoo, Illinois
1846-1848	Mormon migration to Great Basin
1847	First issue of Frederick Douglass's North Star
1848	Noyes founds Oneida community First women's rights convention at Seneca Falls
1850	Nathaniel Hawthorne's Scarlet Letter
1851	Maine prohibition law Herman Melville's Moby-Dick
1854	Thoreau publishes Walden
1855	Massachusetts bans segregated public schools

Other Names to Know

Henry Clay
Nicholas Biddle
Charles G. Finney
Robert Owen
William Miller
Elizabeth Cady Stanton
Sylvester Graham

Daniel Webster
Alexis de Tocqueville
Mother Ann Lee
Joseph Smith
Abby Kelley
Theodore Dwight Weld

(5) GLOSSARY OF IMPORTANT TERMS

Whigs: party opposing Jackson ("King Andrew I"), their name
    referring to the English parliamentary party opposed to
    royal power

nullification: the states' rights doctrine presented by
    John C. Calhoun of South Carolina that said that a
    state could declare federal legislation null and void

ethnocultural politics: the belief that political participa-
    tion and behavior are affected by one's religious,
    ethnic, and cultural background

millennialism: the religious belief that a thousand-year era (millennium) of perfect peace, harmony, and brotherhood was a prerequisite for the Second Coming of Christ

perfectionism: the religious belief that sin and evil could be eradicated in American society as well as in individuals

Transcendentalism: belief of New England intellectuals that the truths found beyond sense experience in intuition and nature would lead people to self-knowledge and self-reliance and ultimately to the attempted reformation of themselves and society

communitarianism: the creation of utopian communities in which members engaged in various forms of cooperation and sharing of property and responsibility for the well-being of all

spiritualism: psychic phenomenon of the 1830s and 1840s by which humans believed they could communicate with unknown worlds, including the dead

abolitionists: reformers who wanted to end slavery

immediatists: abolitionist disciples of Garrison and Weld who wanted to end slavery immediately

nonresistance: the philosophical pacifist belief opposing all forms of governmental or personal coercion

(6) ENRICHMENT IDEAS

1. After working through the RTP, find and read other foreign visitors' accounts of life in the United States in the 1830s and 1840s. How accurate do you think they were? How would you write about another culture you have seen (or imagined)? What questions would you ask? What limitations would you feel? What cultural assumptions would you bring to your observations?

2. Visit the site of one of the several utopian communities mentioned in the chapter. Many still exist, some even restored as living historical museums. Depending on where you live, you might visit Hopedale or Brook Farm near Boston, Massachusetts; Shaker Villages near Pittsfield, Massachusetts and in Kentucky; Ephrata,

Pennsylvania; Zoar, Ohio; New Harmony, Indiana; the Amana colonies in Iowa, etc. Whether or not you can actually visit the original site, you can research further into one or two particular utopian communities.

3. Imagine yourself as part of the colony. How well would you fit in? What would you and dislike like about life in this community? Write a letter to a friend about it, or write a series of imaginary diary entries about life in the community.

4. You can think about similar questions when visiting other sites, for example, Seneca Falls, or Mormon landmarks in Utah, or a prison asylum built in the mid-nineteenth century. A letter or diary entry could be written about your imagined participation in a Whig campaign picnic in 1840, or a revival or temperance meeting broken up by a mob, or a meeting of Mormons considering migration westward, or the women's rights convention in Seneca Falls.

5. Prepare a diagram showing the development of the American political party system from the 1790s to 1840--specifically party names, leaders, principles, programs, campaign issues, and sources of popular electoral support.

(7) SAMPLE TEST AND EXAMINATION QUESTIONS

Multiple choice: Choose the best answer.

1. The Whig party stood for all of the following programs except
    a. a strong national bank
    b. a protective tariff
    c. the right of nullification
    d. restrictions on Sunday business and drinking

2. Which of the following statements best describes the tone of Jackson's presidency?
    a. the emergence of common people to responsibility in government
    b. strong presidential leadership on issues and positions of personal importance to Jackson
    c. unyielding presidential leadership to the principles long clearly identified with the Democratic party
    d. negative leadership, relying on the "kitchen cabinet" to run most executive affairs

3. Jackson defeated John Quincy Adams in 1828 because
   a. Clay's candidacy split the votes Adams should have received
   b. Adams was such an intellectual that the voters did not understand him
   c. voters were so outraged at the attacks on Rachel Jackson that many voted against Adams
   d. Jackson carefully prepared for the election, building a sectionally diverse coalition of support

4. Jacksonian Democrats
   a. supported the concentration of economic power in new corporations
   b. opposed federal government support for public education
   c. were basically advocates of national rather than state sovereignty
   d. encouraged abolitionist criticisms of slavery

5. The Whigs used Democratic campaign techniques against Van Buren in winning the presidential election in
   a. 1832
   b. 1836
   c. 1840
   d. 1844

6. The U.S. Bank performed all of the following services except
   a. shifting government funds to different parts of the country
   b. moderating and regulating state banking activities
   c. issuing large quantities of paper money to stimulate purchasing power
   d. buying and selling government bonds

7. The nullification crisis was resolved when
   a. Jackson sent federal troops to Charleston
   b. popular support for Jackson's threat of force and the compromise tariff isolated South Carolina
   c. Calhoun apologized and resigned as vice-president
   d. Van Buren secured passage of the Tariff of Abominations

8. The removal of the Cherokee Indians was justified by all of the following except
   a. Jackson's argument that the Cherokee could not survive living among whites
   b. Jackson's argument that they were subject to Georgia State laws

c. John Marshall's argument that the Indians' case was "repugnant to the Constitution"
d. white Georgians' arguments that they needed more land for cotton

9. The Whig party had strong support from all of the following except
a. New England
b. small Catholic farmers
c. temperance and other moralistic reformers
d. large cotton planters with a national vision

10. The primary cause of the reform impulse in America in the 1830s was
a. the influx of Catholic European immigrants
b. religious revivalism and socioeconomic changes
c. northern opposition to slavery
d. the building of the Erie Canal

11. The Finney revivals were characterized by
a. the idea that ministers were agents who could cause a revival
b. the idea that revivals were signs of divine intervention
c. extensive drinking during the lengthy meetings
d. an emphasis on reason in seeing one's way to conversion

12. Utopian communities collapsed for all of the following reasons except
a. individualism
b. poor leadership and admissions policies
c. external hostility
d. diversified economies

13. Black and white abolitionists
a. did not work well together because of white paternalism
b. supported each other well despite occasional disagreements
c. worked together only in battling race discrimination in the North but not slavery in the South
d. ignored each other because of the fear of mob violence

14. The concerns of the women's rights movement in the 1840s included all of the following except
a. the right to vote
b. the right of free speech
c. better working conditions
d. equal pay for equal work

127

15. Temperance reformers
    a. focused exclusively on the moral suasion tactic that drinking was a sin
    b. were split between advocates of moderation and total abstinence
    c. succeeded in passing a prohibition amendment before the Civil War
    d. were led by women who hoped to leave abusive husbands

Matching:

Match the person in column A with the appropriate religious or reform concern in column B.

A	B
____ 1. Dorothea Dix	a. antislavery and women's rights
____ 2. William Miller	b. Oneida colony
____ 3. Abby Kelley	c. public education
____ 4. Theodore Dwight Weld	d. Shakers
____ 5. David Ruggles	e. treatment of the insane
____ 6. Martin Delany	f. abolitionism and temperance
____ 7. Ralph Waldo Emerson	g. excessive federal power
____ 8. Horace Mann	h. secular utopian communities
____ 9. Sylvester Graham	i. Black nationalist colonization
____ 10. Joseph Smith	j. northern racial discrimination
____ 11. John H. Noyes	k. Walden
____ 12. Robert Owen	l. Second Coming of Christ
____ 13. Ann Lee	m. diet and sexual restraint
____ 14. Henry David Thoreau	n. self-reliance
____ 15. John C. Calhoun	o. Mormonism

Essays

1. Trace the changing development of the American political party system (and political culture) from 1824 to 1840.

2. Discuss the various dilemmas and problems of reformers, with specific references to the temperance, abolitionist, and women's rights movements.

3. Show the relationship between women's rights and abolitionism.

4. Discuss both the differences and the similarities of Jacksonian politics and social reform.

5. Discuss the many reasons why Americans in the 1830s turned to religion, revivalism, utopianism, and reform. Which approach do you think brought individuals the most satisfaction that they had effectively reshaped their world? Did any? Support your essay with evidence from the chapter.

Identify and Interpret: Quotation
(that is, state who, what, where, when, and why significant)

The history of mankind is a history of repeated injuries and usurpations on the part of man toward woman, having in direct object the establishment of an absolute tyranny over her. To prove this, let facts be submitted to a candid world.

He has never permitted her to exercise her inalienable right to the elective franchise.

He has compelled her to submit to laws, in the formation of which she had no voice.

He has withheld from her rights which are given to the most ignorant and degraded men--both natives and foreigners.

Identify and Interpret: Chart

(that is, first, study the chart and describe what it shows; second, analyze the chart by explaining some of the reasons behind the patterns you see; third, assess the larger significance of the chart)

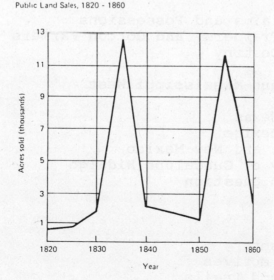

Public Land Sales, 1820 - 1860

Source. U. S. Bureau of Census

14

Moving West

Lewis Cass presents an optimistic picture of what the westward movement represented for the nation. The experiences of Henry Judah and Thomas Gibson in the Mexican War suggest the underside of westward expansion, as do Mary Gibson's worried letters to her husband.

Probing the Trans-Mississippi West

> Foreign Claims and Possessions
> Traders, Trappers, and Cotton Farmers
> Manifest Destiny

Winning the Trans-Mississippi West

> Annexing Texas
> War with Mexico
> California and New Mexico
> The Treaty of Guadalupe Hidalgo
> The Oregon Question

Going West

> The Emigrants
> Migrants' Motives
> The Overland Trails

Living on the Frontier

> The Agricultural Frontier
> The Mining Frontier
> The Mormon Frontier
> The Urban Frontier

Cultures In Conflict

> Confronting the Plains Tribes
> The Fort Laramie Council
> Overwhelming the Mexicans

Conclusion: Fruits of Manifest Destiny

(2) SIGNIFICANT THEMES AND HIGHLIGHTS

1. As the contrasting views of Lewis Cass, Henry Judah, and the Gibsons make clear, the story of the trans-Mississippi West in the nineteenth century is not just the story of the acquisition of territory but also of the experience of thousands of ordinary citizens who fought for new lands or who migrated to the frontier.

2. The chapter emphasizes the use of personal documents, especially the diaries written by men and women on the Overland Trail, in reconstructing historical realities.

3. The political and military events that led to the successful acquisition of western lands came at the expense of Native Americans and Mexicans. The events of this period are presented not only through the eyes of white emigrants but also from the perspective of these two groups.

4. Lewis Cass's attitudes and ideas exemplify the point of view and rhetoric of expansionists who advocated the acquisition of new territories.

131

(3) LEARNING GOALS

Familiarity with Basic Knowledge

After reading this chapter, you should be able to:

1. Define Manifest Destiny.

2. List the sequence of events resulting in the acquisition of Texas, New Mexico, California, and Oregon and locate on a map and date the major territorial acquisitions of the United States between 1803 and 1853.

3. Describe the typical emigrant and three motives leading to the decision to migrate to the Far West.

4. List four ways in which white emigration affected the livelihood of Plains Indians.

5. Explain the terms of the Laramie Council agreements and assess their impact on red-white relations.

6. Contrast the experience of Mexican-Americans in Texas, New Mexico, and California.

Practice in Historical Thinking Skills

After reading this chapter you should be able to:

1. Discuss the United States's policies toward the Plains Indians, placing those events in the context of Indian-white relations until the early 1850s.

2. Compare and contrast opportunities on the mining and farming frontiers.

3. Analyze the role of men and women on the Overland Trail.

(4) IMPORTANT DATES AND NAMES TO KNOW

1803-1806   Lewis and Clark expedition

1818   U.S.-British treaty on joint occupation of Oregon

1819   Spain cedes Florida to the United States and sets Transcontinental boundary of the Louisiana Purchase

1821-1840   Indian removals

132

1821	Mexican independence from Spain Opening of Santa Fe Trail Stephen Austin leads American settlement of Texas
1829	Georgia revokes Cherokee rights
1830	Mexico abolishes slavery in Texas
1836	Texas declares independence The Alamo and Battle of San Jacinto
1840s	Emigrant crossings of Overland Trail
1844	James Polk elected president
1845	Term _Manifest Destiny_ coined United States annexes Texas and sends troops to the Rio Grande; attempts to buy Mexico
1846	Mexico declares defensive war United States declares war and takes Santa Fe Resolution of Oregon question
1847	Attack on Vera Cruz and Mexico City Mormon migration to Utah begins
1848	Treaty of Guadalupe Hidalgo
1849	California gold rush begins
1850	California admitted to Union
1851	Fort Laramie Treaty
1853	Gadsden Purchase
1862	Homestead Act

Other Names to Know

Sam Houston	Antonio López de Santa Anna
Zachary Taylor	John Slidell
Nicholas Trist	

(5) GLOSSARY OF IMPORTANT TERMS

manifest destiny: the belief in the political, religious, and
    cultural superiority of American civilization, giving
    Americans an inherent right to the continent and "true
    title" to its lands

emigrant: term used to describe Americans moving to western
    frontiers

polygamy: a form of marriage in which a husband has more than
    one wife; believed by nineteenth-century Mormons to be
    divinely sanctioned

(6) ENRICHMENT IDEAS

1. The RTP gives examples of diaries and personal
    documents written on the Overland Trail and suggests
    that men and women differed in the content and style
    of what they wrote in their diaries and journals.
    Many diaries have been collected and published. Read
    some of them. What seem to be the typical daily
    concerns of men? Of women? What can you conclude
    about the nature of trail life? What work was
    involved in moving west? What can you learn about
    family and social life through the diaries? Finally,
    do you find differences between journals written by
    men and those written by women? How do you connect
    these materials with the cult of domesticity and the
    idea of separate spheres for men and women?

2. The letters of many of the young men who participated
    in the gold rush are found in printed collections.
    Some may also be on file with your local historical
    society, as the men wrote letters to friends and
    family at home. What picture of mining life can you
    form from these personal documents? How much
    opportunity was there in the mining West as reflected
    in these letters? Did the writers have reasonable
    expectations of their future? What can you tell
    about family life and the social character of mining
    life through reading the letters?

3. In some parts of the United States (Alaska, the
    West), a later frontier period is still fresh in the
    memories of older residents. This provides an
    excellent opportunity for an oral history.

4. On an outline map of the United States, draw in and
    date the major territorial acquisitions between 1803
    and 1853 and the major overland trails and important
    junctions.

(7) SAMPLE TEST AND EXAMINATION QUESTIONS

Multiple choice: Choose the best answer.

1. Which of the following groups is not matched with the appropriate area?
   a. Five Civilized Tribes and the Oklahoma Territory
   b. settlers and squatters and Texas
   c. fur trappers and traders and the Rocky Mountain region
   d. New England shippers and New Mexico

2. The expression Manifest Destiny refers to
   a. the title of a journal published in the 1840s
   b. a speech made by Lewis Cass
   c. the Puritan belief of the uniqueness of the American experience
   d. a belief that because of the superiority of its institutions, Americans should control the North American continent

3. The Transcontinental Treaty of 1819
   a. clearly indicated that Texas belonged to the United States
   b. excluded Texas as part of the United States
   c. made clear that Texas had been part of the Louisiana Purchase
   d. none of the above

4. The Mexican government invited American settlers to Texas
   a. because they feared Texas was weak and needed settlers
   b. because they wanted to gain converts for the Catholic church
   c. because they hoped to see the introduction of American law in this area
   d. because they wanted the labor of black slaves there

5. Texas did not join the Union in 1837
   a. because Texans were still fighting the Mexicans for their independence
   b. because Texans wished to have their own independent republic
   c. because many northerners, fearful of the expansion of slavery, opposed annexation
   d. because Jackson refused to take the advice of his "kitchen cabinet"

6. Polk's objectives in the conflict with Mexico
   included
   a. obtaining California
   b. obtaining New Mexico
   c. settling the boundary of Texas at the Rio Grande
   d. all of the above

7. The war with Mexico
   a. was complicated by the Oregon question
   b. was clearly Mexico's fault
   c. ended in 1848
   d. was popular throughout the United States

8. The acquisition of the Oregon country gave the United
   States land in the Northwest
   a. up to the line 54° 40' north latitude
   b. up to the 49th parallel
   c. around San Francisco
   d. all of the above

9. Most overland emigrants traveled
   a. with strangers
   b. with relatives and friends
   c. with people of their own religion
   d. alone

10. The overland trip to Oregon
    a. was so expensive that only the rich could go west
    b. was so cheap that virtually anyone could become
       an emigrant
    c. cost a substantial amount, making the trip
       possible only for middle-class Americans
    d. cost far more than making the trip by sea

11. On the mining frontier,
    a. most miners struck it rich
    b. most people expected to make a pile and build
       expensive houses in the West
    c. miners who failed to get rich quick soon became
       wage earners
    d. prostitutes were courteously treated because
       there were so few women

12. In Utah,
    a. most families were polygamous
    b. Mormon men usually had more than two wives
    c. polygamous wives frequently tried to escape
    d. few families practiced polygamy

13. The Native Americans of the Great Plains
    a. fiercely attacked the emigrants from the beginning
    b. at first fought one another as much as they did white emigrants
    c. provided buffalo barbecues for emigrants passing through their lands
    d. saw no threat from white emigration

14. All of the following are true about the Fort Laramie Council except that it
    a. drew tribal boundaries
    b. secured promises from some of those present to stay within tribal boundaries
    c. succeeded in firmly establishing the reservation policy
    d. gave Native Americans presents and other forms of compensation

15. The Treaty of Guadalupe Hidalgo
    a. assured former Mexicans that they would enjoy the rights of citizens
    b. promised the protection of their property
    c. seemed to legitimate land grants made by Mexico
    d. all of the above

Identify and show a relationship between each of the following pairs.

mining frontier	and	bandidos
Fort Laramie Council	and	"fifty-four forty or fight"
Manifest Destiny	and	the Trail of Tears
Treaty of Guadalupe Hidalgo	and	Lewis Cass
Overland Trail	and	the Homestead Act

Essays

1. "Manifest Destiny was a policy for whites only." Discuss with specific evidence to support your main points.

2. Although the westward movement may not have realized dreams of opportunity, the fact of emigration did help keep American ideals alive. Write an essay either agreeing or disagreeing with the statement.

3. Analyze the myths and realities of popular images of the American West.

137

Map Question

Locate the following on the accompanying map.

1. The "Trail of Tears"
2. Oregon and California trails
3. Texas Republic, 1836-1845
4. Sioux and Cheyenne lands
5. Sutter's Fort, California
6. Mormon Trail's end, Salt Lake City
7. Rio Grande
8. Colorado River
9. Territory acquired under the Treaty of Guadalupe Hidalgo, 1848

10. Gadsden Purchase
11. Santa Fe Trail
12. Oregon country acquisition, 1846
13. San Francisco
14. Hopi and Navaho lands
15. Black belt
16. Erie Canal

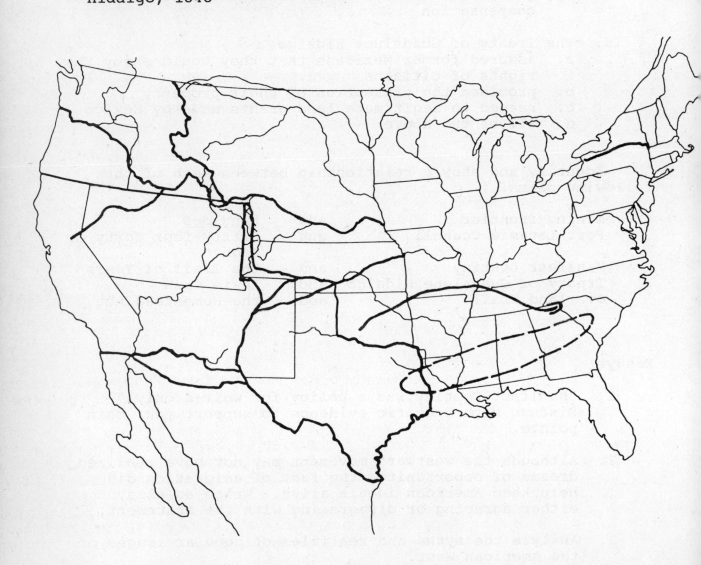

15
The Union in Peril

(1) CHAPTER OUTLINE

As Abraham Lincoln awaits the election returns in November 1860, three other Americans--Robert Allston, a South Carolina slave owner; Frederick Douglass, an escaped slave; and Michael Luark, an Iowa farmer--also watch the results of the election, each filled with intense concern over how the fate of the nation would affect his own.

Slavery in the Territories

Free Soil or Constitutional Protection?
Popular Sovereignty and the Election of 1848
The Compromise of 1850
Consequences of Compromise

Political Disintegration

The Apathetic Election of 1852
The Kansas-Nebraska Act
Expansionist "Young America"
Nativism, Know-Nothings, and Republicans

Kansas and the Two Cultures

Competing for Kansas
"Bleeding Kansas"
Northern Views and Visions
The Southern Perspective

Polarization and the Road to War

      The Dred Scott Case
      Douglas and the Democrats
      Lincoln and the Illinois Debates
      John Brown's Raid
      The Election of 1860

The Divided House Falls

      Secession and Uncertainty
      Lincoln and Fort Sumter

Conclusion: The "Irrepressible Conflict"

(2) SIGNIFICANT THEMES AND HIGHLIGHTS

1.   The heightened tensions surrounding the 1860 election and suggested by the anecdote indicate the central place the Civil War occupies in American history. The causes of the war that dissolved the Union, therefore, are crucial to an understanding of America's history. The causes reflect the interrelationship of politics, emotions, and sectional culture.

2.   Historians have long debated, without resolution, the causes of the Civil War. This chapter focuses on four developments of the period between 1848 and 1861, each an important cause of war. The chapter weaves these developments together in an interpretive narrative account of both the events and the cultural values behind the events. The student is left to decide how the four causes interacted to bring about the war and which, if any, were more important than others.

3.   Events in Kansas in 1855 and 1856 are highlighted as a specific microscopic illustration bringing together many of the forces that led Americans to secession and civil war in 1861.

4.   The primary focus in this chapter is on national political developments involving nationally known figures because the Civil War was, after all, fundamentally a political event. Nevertheless, the chapter includes the comments of ordinary Americans, most frequently those of two figures from earlier chapters, runaway slave Frederick Douglass and South

140

Carolina rice planter Robert Allston, as they
observed the events of the 1850s leading to the
outbreak of civil war.

(3) LEARNING GOALS

Familiarity with Basic Knowledge

After reading this chapter, you should be able to:

1. Explain three or four proposals for dealing with the
   territories acquired in the Mexican War and the
   five provisions of the Compromise of 1850.

2. Describe the breakdown of political parties in the
   early 1850s, explaining the disappearance of old
   parties and the emergence of new ones.

3. Outline the course of the Kansas-Nebraska Act and how
   it affected politics and sectional animosities in the
   mid-1850s.

4. Explain America's expansionist interest in Latin
   America.

5. Show how the events in Kansas in 1855 and 1856, the
   Dred Scott case, the emotional events of 1859-1860,
   and the election of Lincoln led to the secession
   crisis and the outbreak of the Civil War.

Practice in Historical Thinking Skills

After reading this chapter, you should be able to:

1. Describe the differing cultural values of the South
   and North and each section's view of the other, and
   explain how these cultural differences helped lead to
   civil war.

2. Explain the development and significance of each of
   the four causes of the Civil War, citing four or five
   specific examples for each.

3. Evaluate the four causes, indicating which ones (or
   one) you think were most significant in explaining
   why the North and South went to war in 1861.

(4) IMPORTANT DATES AND NAMES TO KNOW

1820	Missouri Compromise
1832	South Carolina Nullification crisis
1835-1840	Intensification of abolitionist attacks on slavery Violent retaliatory attacks on abolitionists
1840	Liberty party formed
1846	Wilmot Proviso
1848	Free-Soil party founded Zachary Taylor elected president
1850	Compromise of 1850, including Fugitive Slave Act
1850-1854	"Young America" movement
1851	Women's rights convention in Akron, Ohio
1852	Harriet Beecher Stowe publishes best-selling Uncle Tom's Cabin Franklin Pierce elected president
1853	Gadsden Purchase
1854	Ostend Manifesto Kansas-Nebraska Act repeals Missouri Compromise Formation of Republican and Know-Nothing parties
1855	Walt Whitman, Leaves of Grass
1855-1856	Julia Lovejoy, David Atchison, and thousands of others pour into Kansas, creating months of turmoil and violence
1856	John Brown's massacre in Kansas Sumner-Brooks incident in Washington James Buchanan elected president
1857	Dred Scott decision legalizes slavery in territories Lecompton constitution in Kansas
1858	Lincoln-Douglas debates
1859	John Brown's raid at Harpers Ferry
1860	Democratic party splits Four-party campaign Abraham Lincoln elected president

1860-1861	Secession of seven southern states
1861	Confederate States of America founded Attack on Fort Sumter begins Civil War

Other Names to Know

Sojourner Truth	Stephen Douglas
William Walker	Frederick Douglass
William Marcy	William Seward

(5) GLOSSARY OF IMPORTANT TERMS

popular sovereignty: the doctrine that left the decision
    whether a state would enter the Union slave or free up
    to the territorial legislature representing the people
    of that territory

nativism: antiforeign feelings and behavior (especially
    against Irish Catholic immigrants) expressed by native-
    born Americans

Young America: a term describing proud, confident, highly
    nationalistic, expansionist Americans in the early 1850s

(6) ENRICHMENT IDEAS

1. RTP: Read further into the Senate debates over the
Compromise of 1850, analyzing and discussing the
style and arguments of various speeches, especially
the complete texts of those by Clay, Webster,
Calhoun, and Seward.

2. It is 1855. Create a dialogue between two recent
migrants to Kansas, one from Massachusetts and one
from Missouri. Put them in an appropriate setting
and provide an end to their conversation, but focus
mainly on how each reveals his or her sectional
origins and views and how each sees the other.

3. You are Lincoln in the winter of 1860-1861. What
would you do? You are Frederick Douglass in the same
winter. What would you do? You are Robert Allston
at the same time. What would you do? Why? What do
you think would happen?

(7) SAMPLE TEST AND EXAMINATION QUESTIONS

Multiple choice: Choose the best answer.

1. According to the author of Chapter 15, the most
   pervasive underlying cause of the Civil War was
   a. slavery
   b. political blundering
   c. abolitionist agitation
   d. economic differences

2. The Wilmot Proviso stated that
   a. Congress should protect slavery in the
      territories acquired from Mexico
   b. the people of those territories should decide for
      themselves whether to permit slavery
   c. slavery should be prohibited in these territories
   d. slavery should be prohibited only north of the
      line $36^{\circ}30'$

3. The Compromise of 1850 included all of the following
   provisions except
   a. a stronger Fugitive Slave Act
   b. the admission of California as a free state
   c. the abolition of slavery and the slave trade in
      the District of Columbia
   d. the organization of New Mexico and Utah according
      to the principle of popular sovereignty

4. Of those blacks arrested in the North under the
   Fugitive Slave Act, most
   a. were able to purchase their freedom
   b. were returned to the South
   c. escaped and fled to Canada
   d. were rescued by sympathetic whites

5. All of the following were Democrats except
   a. Franklin Pierce
   b. Stephen Douglas
   c. James Buchanan
   d. Millard Fillmore

6. Party distinctiveness and loyalty decreased in the
   early 1850s because of
   a. improving economic conditions
   b. the upsurge of expansionist fervor
   c. Fillmore's friendship with Douglas
   d. the lasting success of the Compromise of 1850

7. The Kansas-Nebraska Act
    a. settled the question of slavery in the
        territories
    b. unified the Democratic party
    c. guaranteed Douglas the presidential nomination in
        1856
    d. seriously weakened Douglas' support from northern
        Democrats

8. The Know-Nothing party advocated
    a. a lengthy period before immigrants could become
        citizens
    b. the abolition of slavery
    c. government regulation of Catholic parochial
        schools
    d. all of the above

9. The Republican party in 1860
    a. stood for the principle of popular sovereignty
    b. opposed the extension of slavery into the
        territories
    c. advocated the abolition of slavery
    d. promised not to interfere with southern slavery
        but supported equal rights for free blacks in the
        North

10. Which of the following is in the correct chrono-
    logical order?
    a. Kansas-Nebraska Act, Fugitive Slave Act, Dred
        Scott case
    b. Fugitive Slave Act, Kansas-Nebraska Act, Dred
        Scott case
    c. Fugitive Slave Act, Dred Scott case,
        Kansas-Nebraska Act
    d. Dred Scott case, Kansas-Nebraska Act, Fugitive
        Slave Act

11. The Ostend Manifesto claimed Cuba as a natural part
    of the United States because of
    a. geographic proximity and mutual economic
        interests
    b. historic ties and treaty obligation
    c. the influence of the United Fruit Company
    d. all of the above

12. Which of the following statements of the southern
    perspective is not true?
    a. Northerners were ill-mannered, mean, and
        materialistic.
    b. The South was a genteel and orderly society
        guided by gentlemen planters.

145

c. Slavery was an unfortunate but necessary evil
    resulting from high northern tariffs.
d. Southerners revered local self-government as a
    basic republican right.

13. According to the Dred Scott decision,
    a. the Compromise of 1850 was declared
        unconstitutional
    b. free Negroes but not slaves had the right to sue
        in federal courts
    c. Dred Scott was entitled to his freedom because he
        had lived in a free state
    d. Dred Scott had no right to sue and was denied his
        freedom

14. Of the options facing him in the winter of 1861-1862,
    Lincoln favored
    a. compromising with the secessionist states
    b. letting secessionist states "go in peace"
    c. risking war by upholding the laws of the land and
        protecting federal property
    d. going to war in a daring first strike against the
        secessionist states

15. Which of the following is in the correct chrono-
    logical order?
    a. John Brown's raid, secession of South Carolina,
        Lincoln's election, Fort Sumter
    b. Lincoln's election, secession of South Carolina,
        John Brown's raid, Fort Sumter
    c. John Brown's raid, Lincoln's election, secession
        of South Carolina, Fort Sumter
    d. Lincoln's election, John Brown's raid, secession
        of South Carolina, Fort Sumter

    Date the following events and place them in the correct
chronological order:

                Dred Scott decision
                Kansas-Nebraska Act
                Fort Sumter
                Compromise of 1850
                end of Mexican War
                "bleeding Kansas"
                Missouri Compromise

Essays

1. Explain your view of the causes of the Civil War, citing appropriate specific evidence to defend your explanation.

2. Select three or four specific events and developments in the 1850s that you think were the most significant in causing the Civil War. Defend your choices and explain why you think other events and developments were less significant.

3. Construct a dialogue between a New England migrant and a Missouri slaveholder over whether Kansas should become a slave or free state. Use your imagination in setting the scene (and the outcome), but focus your primary attention on how each person reflects his or her sectional view and how that section viewed the other.

Identify and Interpret: Cartoon
(that is, state who, what, where, when, and why significant)

16

The Union Severed

(1) CHAPTER OUTLINE

A young northern man, Arthur Carpenter, begs his parents
for permission to join the army and wins their consent. A
southern Presbyterian preacher, George Eagleton of Tennessee,
feels compelled to enlist and leaves his sorrowful wife,
Ethie, and their baby to go to war.

Organizing to Fight the War

> The Balance of Resources
> The Border States
> Challenges of War
> Lincoln and Davis

Clashing on the Battlefield, 1861-1862

> War in the East
> War in the West
> Naval Warfare
> Cotton Diplomacy
> Common Problems, Novel Solutions
> Political Dissension

The Tide Turns, 1863-1865

> The Emancipation Proclamation
> Unanticipated Consequences of War
> Changing Military Strategies

Changes Wrought by War

Conclusion: Union Triumphant

(2) SIGNIFICANT THEMES AND HIGHLIGHTS

1. This chapter attempts to provide a coherent picture of the Civil War as a military and diplomatic event, but, as the stories of Arthur Carpenter and the Eagletons suggest, the chapter emphasizes the impact of the war on the lives of ordinary people: soldiers who fought the war and noncombatants behind the lines, such as women like Ethie Eagleton and Emily Harris, slaves, and working-class Americans.

2. In numerous, unanticipated ways, the war transformed northern and southern society. The changes were most dramatic in the South, where by the war's end leaders were contemplating the use of slaves as soldiers and even emancipation. Ironically, although the war was fought to save distinctly different ways of life, the conflict forced both sides to adopt similar measures and to become more alike.

3. In the North, the war was fought to save the Union. Only gradually did goals shift to include the emancipation of slaves. Lincoln's racial leadership is emphasized despite his inability to reduce racism significantly in northern society.

4. The chapter continually shows the contrasts between northern and southern resources, leadership, military strategy, wartime political and economic problems and solutions, and the impact of the war on race relations, women, daily life, and other features of the home front.

(3) LEARNING GOALS

Familiarity with Basic Knowledge

After reading this chapter, you should be able to:

1. Compare and contrast the balance of resources in the North and the South at the war's beginning and its end.

2. State the significance of the border states to both the Union and the Confederacy.

3. List the various manpower and financial measures taken by the Confederate and Union governments during the course of the war.

4. Describe the origins, purposes, and provisions of the Emancipation Proclamation.

5. List the ways in which Lincoln and Davis expanded presidential powers.

6. Describe the participation of women in the war.

Practice in Historical Thinking Skills

After reading this chapter, you should be able to:

1. Discuss the social political and economic impact of the war on both societies and show how the South became increasingly similar to the North.

2. Analyze the impact of the Emancipation Proclamation on the course of the war and on race relations.

3. Analyze why the North won the war and the South lost it.

(4) IMPORTANT DATES AND NAMES TO KNOW

1861 Lincoln calls up state militias and suspends habeas corpus
First Battle of Bull Run
Union blockades the South

1862 Battles at Shiloh, Bull Run, and Antietam
Monitor and Virginia battle
First black regiment authorized by Union
South institutes military draft
Union issues greenbacks

Morrill Tariff
Morrill (land-grant colleges) Act
Pacific Railroad Act
Homestead Act

1863   Lincoln issues Emancipation Proclamation
        First Conscription Act by Union
        Battles of Gettysburg and Vicksburg
        Union Banking Act
        Southern tax laws and impressment act
        New York draft riots, Southern food riots

1864   Sherman's march through Georgia
        Lincoln reelected

1865   Lee surrenders at Appomattox
        Lincoln assassinated
        Andrew Johnson becomes president
        Congress passes Thirteenth Amendment

Other Names to Know

Robert E. Lee   William Seward
Henri Jomini   Ulysses S. Grant
Jefferson Davis   Salmon Chase
George McClellan   Horace Greeley
General William T. Sherman

(5) GLOSSARY OF IMPORTANT TERMS

cotton diplomacy: the belief in the South that cotton would
    generate support for the Confederate cause in Europe

bounty: the fee, ranging from $800 to $1000, paid to
    individuals by northern communities who wished to fill
    their military quota outside of their own communities

copperheads: Northern Democrats who wished for a peaceful and
    speedy end to the war. The Republican press struck them
    with the label of the deadly snakes

impressment: the confiscation or taking of private property
    for the war effort

radicals: group of Republicans, never very many, who wished
    not only for the emancipation of the slaves but also for
    fundamental changes in southern society after the war

Confederacy: the name given to the new southern nation
    between 1861 and 1865

(6) ENRICHMENT IDEAS

1. Study a volume of photographs of the Civil War taken by Mathew Brady and others. Choose two or three photographs and study them closely. First, describe what they contain: What objects are in each? What people? How are they dressed? What are their expressions (faces and bodies)? What appears to be the relation between them? Then draw some conclusions: What atmosphere has been created? Why were the photos taken and for whom? What can you learn about the Civil War by studying photos of the conflict? What are the limitations of this kind of historical evidence? How has the technological level of the equipment shaped photography?

2. Find some letters or diaries written by a participant in the Civil War. You may have some in your family, or check your college or university library archives; most historical societies will have manuscript resources of this kind. If all else fails, there are good printed collections of letters and diaries written by soldiers. You might also want to look at materials written by people at home. What kinds of experience does your writer describe? What seems important to him or her? What understanding of the war does your writer have?

3. If a Civil War battlefield is nearby, visit it. Imagine yourself a typical soldier writing home with news of that battle. What would you say?

(7) SAMPLE TEST AND EXAMINATION QUESTIONS

Multiple choice: Choose the best answer.

1. Early opponents of the war included all of the following except
   a. free blacks in the North
   b. white yeoman farmers who owned no slaves
   c. Irish immigrants
   d. northern Democrats from the Midwest

2. In 1861, Lincoln called up state militias for
   a. three months
   b. six months
   c. one year
   d. three years

3. In 1861, the South had the advantage of
   a. a slave population that could be used in the war effort
   b. substantial agricultural resources
   c. a larger population of males than the North
   d. an adequate railroad system

4. All of the following border states eventually joined the Confederacy except
   a. Virginia
   b. Tennessee
   c. Kentucky
   d. Arkansas

5. In the early days of the war, Lincoln
   a. scrupulously respected individual civil rights
   b. revoked General Fremont's emancipation proclamation in Missouri
   c. ordered the immediate recruitment of black soldiers
   d. decided against a naval blockade of the South

6. The first battle of Bull Run indicated
   a. that the southern army was on the way to becoming a professional fighting force
   b. that northern commanders had a well-developed strategic plan to defeat the South
   c. that a volunteer army would be sufficient for the conflict
   d. the deficiencies of short-term enlistment

7. Cotton diplomacy failed because
   a. European powers believed the South could not win the war
   b. Europe was in a depression and could not buy cotton
   c. there was a cotton glut in Europe
   d. European nations were not interested in the conflict

8. The war was financed on both sides mostly by
   a. government borrowing
   b. taxation
   c. foreign loans
   d. printing paper money

9. In the South,
   a. all soldiers were drafted
   b. about a third of the Confederate army was conscripted
   c. many slaves served as soldiers
   d. only slave owners served in the army

10. In the North, moderate and conservative Republicans
    a. favored the emancipation of slaves
    b. supported the use of blacks as soldiers
    c. hoped for sweeping social and economic changes in
       the South
    d. feared all of the above

11. The Emancipation Proclamation technically freed
    a. slaves in the border states
    b. free blacks only
    c. slaves in areas conquered by Union armies
    d. slaves in unconquered parts of the Confederacy

12. The Confederate government
    a. honored the concept of states' rights
    b. honored the principle of private property
    c. favored conscription and taxation
    d. favored using emancipated slaves as soldiers

13. The demands of war produced
    a. deflation
    b. inflation
    c. increases in real wages
    d. heavy unemployment

14. Grant's final campaign
    a. was intended to secure the Mississippi
    b. was aimed at luring Lee into one final decisive
       battle
    c. was aimed at the total destruction of all
       Confederate armies and resources
    d. depended on guerrilla warfare

15. The Civil War
    a. was a tremendous boon to northern industry
    b. stimulated northern manufacturing only in certain
       war-related industries
    c. had surprisingly little effect on industry
    d. created financial chaos and thus disrupted
       industry

   Identify and show a relationship between each of the
following pairs.

    Emily Harris   and   Arthur Carpenter
    Emancipation Proclamation   and   Antietam
    Jefferson Davis   and   Greenbacks
    General William Sherman   and   Henri Jomini

Essays

1. Think about and write essays on items 1-3 found in "Learning Goals" in the section <u>Practice in Historical Thinking Skills</u>.

2. "If one is to understand the Civil War, it is important to realize that it was not fought to end slavery." Develop an essay showing the extent to which you agree or disagree with this statement.

3. "Lincoln's masterful leadership was the main ingredient of northern victory." To what extent do you agree or disagree with this statement?

Identify and Interpret: Quotation
(that is, state who, what, where, when, and why significant)

With malice toward none; with charity for all; with firmness in the right, as God gives us to see the right, let us strive on to finish the work we are in; to bind up the nation's wounds; to care for him who shall have borne the battle, and for his widow, and his orphan--to do all which may achieve and cherish a just, and a lasting peace, among ourselves, and with all nations.

Map Question:

Locate the following on the accompanying map.

1. Washington, D.C.
2. the eleven Confederate States of America
3. Fort Sumter
4. Antietam and Bull Run
5. Shiloh
6. Vicksburg
7. Gettysburg
8. Sherman's route to the sea
9. Montgomery, Alabama
10. the four border states remaining in the Union
11. Appomattox
12. new state seceding from Virginia 1863

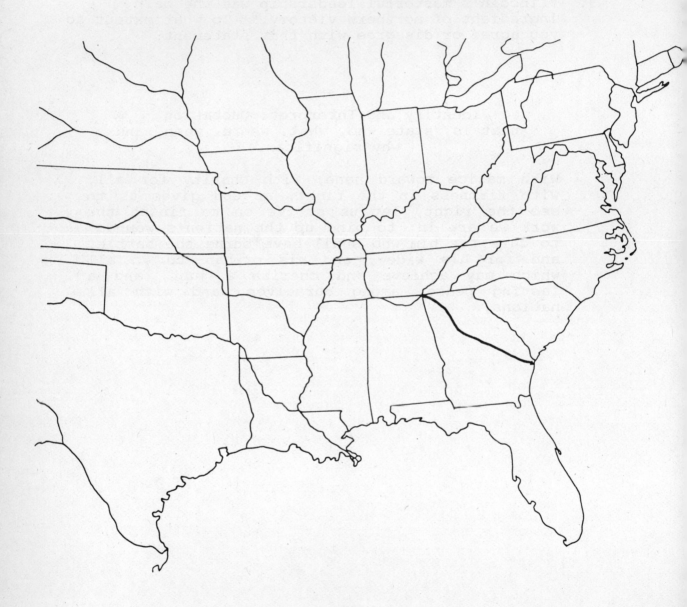

17

The Union Reconstructed

(1) CHAPTER OUTLINE

Adele and Elizabeth Allston fearfully return to their plantations after the war. At Nightingale Hall, they have a joyous reunion with their former slaves. But at Guendalos, the blacks are defiant, the atmosphere threatening. The morning after the arrival, however, Uncle Jacob, the former black driver, hands the keys to the crop barns over to the women in recognition that they still own the land.

The Bittersweet Aftermath of War

> The United States in 1865
> Hopes Among Freedmen
> The White South's Fearful Response

National Reconstruction

> The Presidential Plan
> Congressional Reconstruction
> The President Impeached
> Congressional Moderation
> Women and the Reconstruction Amendments

Life After Slavery

> The Freedmen's Bureau
> Economic Freedom by Degrees
> Black Self-help Institutions

157

Reconstruction in the States

        Republican Rule
        Violence and "Redemption"
        Reconstruction, Northern Style
        The End of Reconstruction

Conclusion: A Mixed Legacy

(2) SIGNIFICANT THEMES AND HIGHLIGHTS

1. The account of the Allstons' return to their plantations highlights the focus of this chapter. The primary action of the chapter takes place on the old southern plantation and in the freedmen's cabins, not in the halls of Congress and the White House. Rather than emphasizing the political programs and conflicts of Congress and the president, we see the hopes and fears of ordinary persons--both black and white--as they faced their postwar world. Political events, North as well as South in the years between 1865 and 1877, are included, but they are secondary to the psychosocial dynamics of reconstructing new relationships among differing people after the Civil War.

2. As reflected in the opening anecdote, the dreams and aspirations of three groups--white southerners, black freedmen, and white northerners--are introduced and woven together throughout the chapter. The main question of the chapter is, What happens as these three sets of goals come into conflict? Uncle Jacob's return of the keys to the crop barns to the Allston family, a gesture symbolic of ownership, indicates the crucial importance of labor and land to an understanding of the outcome of these conflicting goals. The result was a mixed legacy of human gains and losses.

3. The experiences of the Allston family are concluded in this chapter. Frederick Douglass's astute observations as a black leader continue as those of W. E. B. Du Bois begin.

4. The tragic elements of the Reconstruction, or any other era, are perhaps best represented in literature. Novels and short stories are used in this chapter to capture these human conflicts.

(3) LEARNING GOALS

Familiarity with Basic Knowledge

After reading this chapter, you should be able to:

1. State four or five particular goals of three groups at the end of the Civil War: the freedmen, white southerners, and white northerners.

2. Describe the situation and mood of the country at the end of the Civil War and describe the first programs and actions of southern whites and freedmen as they redefined race relations in 1865.

3. Explain President Johnson's reconstruction program and contrast it with Congress's alternative program.

4. Name and explain three important acts and three constitutional amendments that were part of the Republican reconstruction program.

5. Explain the arrangements for working the land that developed between white landowners and the freedmen and describe the terms of a typical work contract.

6. Describe the character of the Republican state governments in the South during Reconstruction: Who ruled? How well? For how long? How did these governments come to an end?

Practice in Historical Thinking Skills

After reading this chapter, you should be able to:

1. Assess the relationship between the character of national politics during Grant's term of office from 1869 to 1877 and the end of Reconstruction in the South.

2. Show how the diverse goals of the white southerners, freedmen, and white northerners came into conflict and assess to what extent each group achieved its various goals by the end of Reconstruction.

3. Evaluate the respective roles southern and northern whites played in impeding black goals.

(4) IMPORTANT DATES AND NAMES TO KNOW

1865   Civil War ends
         Lincoln assassinated
         Johnson's general amnesty and reconstruction plan
         Racial confusion, widespread hunger, and
         demobilization
         Thirteenth Amendment ratified
         Freedmen's Bureau established

1865-1866   Black codes passed throughout ex-Confederate states
         Repossession of land by whites and signing of
         contracts with freedmen

1866   Freedmen's Bureau bill renewed over Johnson's veto
         Civil Rights Act passed over Johnson's veto
         Southern Homestead Act
         Ku Klux Klan formed
         Tennessee readmitted to Union

1867   Reconstruction Acts passed over Johnson's veto
         Impeachment controversy
         Freedmen's Bureau ends

1868   Impeachment of Johnson fails
         Ulysses S. Grant elected president
         Fourteenth Amendment ratified

1868-1870   Readmission of ten states under congressional plan

1869   Tennessee and Virginia reestablish Democratic party
         control

1870   Fifteenth Amendment ratified

1870-1871   Force and Ku Klux Klan acts passed by Congress
         North Carolina and Georgia reestablish Democratic
         control

1870s-1880s Black "exodusters" migrate to Kansas

1872   General Amnesty Act
         Grant reelected

1873   Texas reestablishes Democratic party control

1874   Alabama and Arkansas reestablish Democratic control

1875   Civil Rights Act
         Mississippi Plan reestablishes Democratic control

1876	Disputed Hayes-Tilden election
1876-1877	South Carolina, Louisiana, and Florida reestablish Democratic party control
1877	Compromise of 1877 Rutherford B. Hayes assumes presidency and ends Reconstruction
1880s	Tenancy and sharecropping prevail in the South Disenfranchisement and segregation of southern blacks begins

Other Names to Know

Edwin Stanton
Jay Gould
Charles Sumner

"Pap" Singleton
General O. O. Howard
Thaddeus Stevens

(5) GLOSSARY OF IMPORTANT TERMS

freedmen: former slaves emancipated by the Thirteenth Amendment

carpetbagger: a derogatory term applied to northerners who settled in the South after the Civil War

scalawag: a derogatory term applied to southern Unionists who supported Republican state governments during Reconstruction

debt slavery/peonage: the economic situation in which tenant farmers or sharecroppers become trapped in perpetual debt because they always owe more to their landlords than they get from the sale of cotton

amnesty: removing blame and punishment for past crimes

radical Republicans: a derogatory term applied to northern Republican politicians who generally wanted not only to punish the ex-Confederate leaders but also to help the freedmen fulfill their goals (overstated term; most Republicans were moderate)

"waving the bloody shirt": a Republican political campaign tactic of reminding voters of the Civil War and the valuable role the Republican party in preserving the Union and defeating the rebellious (Democratic) South

161

exodusters: disillusioned blacks who fled the South in the 1870s and 1880s to settle in all-black towns in the western prairies

redemption: a word used by southerners to describe the return of conservative Democrats to power in southern state governments, thus removing the so-called radical Republicans from power

Grantism: a term describing political corruption and graft in the North in the 1870s

(6) ENRICHMENT IDEAS

1. The RTP, which focuses on the ways in which novels reflect history, includes only a very brief excerpt from two novels about Reconstruction. Consider in a longer excerpt the style and point of view of the authors of the six novels listed below. Which do you think most accurately reflects the historical truth about Reconstruction? Is the most accurate novel-as-history necessarily the best as literature? Based on these excerpts, which novel do you think you would like to read in its entirety, and why?

   Thomas Dixon,   The Clansman
   Albion Tourgee,   A Fool's Errand
   Howard Fast,   Freedom Road
   W. E. B. Du Bois,   Quest of the Silver Fleece
   John De Forest,   Miss Ravenal's Conversion from
                        Secession to Loyalty
   Earnest Gaines,   The Autobiography of Miss Jane
                        Pittman

2. Complete the textbook chart "Conflicting Goals During Reconstruction" for the following groups in 1865 by showing what happened to each group by 1877. How well were each of their earlier goals fulfilled? When you have completed the chart, you are in a position to assess the success of Reconstruction and to understand developments in the South into the twentieth century.

   a. victorious northern radical Republicans
   b. northern moderates (Republicans and Democrats)
   c. old southern planter aristocracy (ex-Confederates)
   d. New "Other South" yeoman farmers and Unionists
   e. black freedmen

3. Write a short story or a series of letters or diary entries describing the typical daily experiences of various persons during Reconstruction. For example, a southern woman, Adele Allston, or her daughter Elizabeth, presiding over a large cotton plantation in the absence of their husband and father who was killed in the war. Or a black family that had been given 40 acres of confiscated land by a northern general during the war and faced a title dispute with and dispossession by the original landowner afterward. Or a poor white family putting their lives together in the changing economic climate and race relationships of the postwar years. Or a Yankee schoolteacher's experiences in a Freedmen's Bureau school in Tennessee. Or a Freedmen's Bureau agent's hectic, overworked, underappreciated daily duties in Mississippi. Read in class and discuss. Notice the clash of unresolved dreams.

(7) SAMPLE TEST AND EXAMINATION QUESTIONS

Multiple choice: Choose the best answer.

1. Which of the following is in the correct order?
   a. Black codes, Fourteenth Amendment, Mississippi Plan
   b. Fourteenth Amendment, Mississippi Plan, Reconstruction Acts
   c. Black codes, Mississippi Plan, Fourteenth Amendment
   d. Mississippi Plan, Black codes, Reconstruction Acts

2. All of the following are true descriptions of the United States in April 1865 except
   a. many southern cities were physically devastated
   b. black ex-slaves were in a confused state of semifreedom
   c. the defeated southern rebels were eager to regain their former lands and laborers
   d. most northerners wanted to punish the southern rebels severely

3. All of the following are true of the freedmen in the first months of emancipation except
   a. they went searching for missing family members
   b. they left the plantation briefly but usually returned to the place and work they knew best

163

c. they showed great interest in getting an
   education
d. they left their masters as soon as possible,
   usually stealing property as an expression of
   revenge

4. Congressional Republicans passed all of the following
   bills except
   a. a land bill granting 40 acres and a mule to black
      Union veterans
   b. a civil rights bill
   c. Reconstruction Acts dividing the South into five
      military districts
   d. a bill extending the Freedmen's Bureau

5. The heart of President Johnson's Reconstruction
   program was
   a. to punish all wealthy ex-Confederates by
      confiscating their land
   b. general amnesty and pardons for most
      ex-Confederates
   c. insistence on passage of the Fourteenth Amendment
   d. a land bill for poor and middle-class southern
      whites

6. The most obvious failure of the Freedmen's Bureau was
   in its role
   a. distributing emergency rations
   b. setting the freedmen up on their own land
   c. setting up schools for the freedmen
   d. facilitating family reunions and marriage and
      work for the freedmen

7. Most Republican politicians in the Reconstruction era
   were motivated by all of the following except
   a. the desire to maintain political power
   b. some idealistic concern for protecting the civil
      rights of the freedmen
   c. a vindictive desire to confiscate rebel land and
      redistribute it among blacks
   d. a concern for securing continued economic growth
      of northern industry

8. Republican state governments in the South were
   a. dominated by blacks
   b. dominated by "carpetbaggers" and "scalawags"
   c. hampered by the fact that federal troops left the
      South so quickly
   d. the most corrupt in the nation

9. State governments in the South during Reconstruction accomplished all of the following except
   a. providing public school systems
   b. approving generous measures for economic rebuilding
   c. liberalizing divorce and penal laws
   d. guaranteeing permanent black suffrage

10. The Democrats returned to power in the South because
    a. the Republicans made such a mess of the tax system
    b. blacks did not receive 40 acres and a mule
    c. secret organizations used violence to drive out Republicans
    d. Grant realized that the Republican party was harming itself by its policies on the state level

11. By the 1870s, the Republican party
    a. was reinforced as the party of moral reform and black rights
    b. became more and more a party representing big business
    c. blocked most transportation schemes
    d. supported women's rights

12. Grant's administration was characterized by
    a. scandals like the Whiskey Ring affair
    b. an excess of democracy
    c. zealous attempts to reduce graft
    d. none of the above

13. The Civil Rights Act of 1875
    a. condemned the Ku Klux Klan for violations of the Fourteenth Amendment
    b. passed the House but was defeated in the Senate
    c. passed both Houses of Congress but was vetoed by the president
    d. was passed by Congress and signed by the president but not really enforced

14. The significance of the election of 1877 was that it
    a. ended Reconstruction
    b. resulted in the removal of the last federal troops from the South
    c. resulted in federal aid for the South
    d. all of the above

15. Which of the following authors is incorrectly matched with his work?
    a. Albion Tourgee--A Fool's Errand
    b. Thomas Dixon, Jr.--The Clansman

c. Henry Adams--<u>Leaves of Grass</u>
d. W. E. B. Dubois--"Of the Coming of John"

Briefly identify and show a relationship between each of the following pairs.

General O. O. Howard   and   Thaddeus Stevens
black codes   and   the Fourteenth Amendment
proclamation of general amnesty and the Reconstruction Acts
freedmen work contracts   and   southern homestead acts
Mississippi Plan of 1875   and   Force Act of 1870-1871
"40 acres and a mule"   and   "peace at any price"
annual wage contract   and   sharecropping

Essays

1. Use items 1-3 under "Practice in Historical Thinking Skills" in the "Learning Goals" section to develop essays.

2. In <u>The Souls of Black Folk</u>, W. E. B. Du Bois wrote: "So the Freedmen's Bureau died, and its child was the Fifteenth Amendment." Discuss, showing how this statement might be interpreted as an apt summary of Reconstruction.

3. In <u>The Souls of Black Folk</u>, W. E. B. Du Bois says: "Negro suffrage ended a civil war by beginning a race feud." Discuss the heritage of Reconstruction. To what extent did the events of that period create a continuing race feud in America, sectional animosity, and patterns of political party allegiance? To what extent do these phenomena still exist? How would you have done better?

ANSWERS TO SAMPLE TEST AND EXAMINATION QUESTIONS *

Chapter 1	Chapter 2	Chapter 3	Chapter 4	Chapter 5
1. a	1. c	1. b	1. a	1. c
2. d	2. b	2. c	2. d	2. a
3. b	3. a	3. d	3. c	3. d
4. b	4. a	4. a	4. d	4. a
5. d	5. b	5. d	5. d	5. b
6. c	6. c	6. a	6. c	6. c
7. d	7. b	7. b	7. c	7. c
8. b	8. d	8. b	8. c	8. b
9. c	9. a	9. b	9. d	9. c
10. a	10. d	10. c	10. a	10. b
11. d	11. c	11. d	11. b	11. d
12. c	12. c	12. d	12. c	12. c
13. c	13. a	13. d	13. d	13. b
14. d	14. d	14. c	14. b	14. d
	15. c	15. a	15. d	15. a
			16. a	

Chapter 6

Multiple Choice

1. a
2. b
3. b
4. a
5. c
6. d
7. c
8. a
9. b
10. b
11. d
12. c
13. d

Order & Dates

1. 1763 End of Seven Years' War
2. 1765 Stamp Act
3. 1773 Boston Tea Party
4. 1775 Lexington and Concord
5. 1776 Declaration of Independence
6. 1777 Battle of Saratoga
7. 1781 Yorktown
8. 1783 Treaty of Paris
9. 1784 Treaty of Fort Stanwix
10. 1787 Constitutional Convention

* Answers to the Quotation and Chart Identifications and the Map
Questions are found at the end of this section.

	Chapter 7 Multiple Choice	Chapter 8 True or False		Chapter 9		Chapter 10

Chapter 7 Multiple Choice	Chapter 8 True or False	Chapter 9	Chapter 10
1. a	1. True	1. c	1. c	1. d
2. b	2. False	2. b	2. c	2. d
3. d	3. True	3. b	3. d	3. c
4. d	4. True	4. c	4. d	4. a
5. a	5. False	5. a	5. b	5. d
6. c	6. True	6. c	6. d	6. b
7. d	7. False	7. d	7. a	7. c
8. c	8. True	8. a	8. b	8. d
9. a	9. False	9. b	9. c	9. a
10. c	10. True	10. d	10. b	10. c
11. d	11. True	11. a	11. b	11. c
12. a	12. True	12. b	12. a	12. c
13. b	13. False	13. c	13. d	13. b
	14. False		14. a	14. a
	15. False		15. d	
	16. True			
	17. False			

Chapter 11	Chapter 12	Chapter 13 Multiple Choice	Chapter 13 Matching	Chapter 14
1. d	1. c	1. c	1. e	1. d
2. b	2. d	2. b	2. l	2. d
3. b	3. a	3. d	3. a	3. b
4. c	4. a	4. b	4. f	4. a
5. d	5. b	5. c	5. j	5. c
6. b	6. a	6. c	6. i	6. d
7. d	7. a	7. b	7. n	7. c
8. a	8. c	8. c	8. c	8. b
9. c	9. b	9. b	9. m	9. b
10. c	10. c	10. b	10. o	10. c
11. b	11. c	11. a	11. b	11. c
12. d	12. b	12. d	12. h	12. d
13. c	13. b	13. b	13. d	13. b
14. c	14. b	14. d	14. k	14. c
15. b	15. c	15. b	15. g	15. d
16. a				
17. c				

Chapter 15		Chapter 16	Chapter 17
Multiple Choice	**Order & Dates**		
1. a	1. 1820 Missouri Compromise	1. a	1. a
2. c	2. 1848 end of Mexican War	2. a	2. d
3. c	3. 1850 Compromise of 1850	3. a	3. d
4. b	4. 1854 Kansas-Nebraska Act	4. c	4. a
5. d	5. 1855-1856 "bleeding" Kansas	5. b	5. b
6. a	6. 1857 Dred Scott decision	6. d	6. b
7. d	7. 1861 Fort Sumter	7. c	7. c
8. a		8. d	8. c
9. b		9. b	9. d
10. b		10. d	10. c
11. a		11. d	11. b
12. c		12. c	12. a
13. d		13. b	13. d
14. c		14. c	14. d
15. c		15. b	15. c

ANSWERS: IDENTIFY AND INTERPRET

Chapter 2 - Quotation

John Winthrop, "A Model of Christian Charity," a sermon delivered on board the _Arbella_ while crossing the Atlantic in 1630. A statement of the importance of a covenant, both among the Puritans and with God, in establishing a model community of saints for others to admire and imitate.

Chapter 3 - Chart: Colonial Population

1. This chart highlights the growth of white and black population between 1640 and 1770. At the beginning of the period, blacks constituted only a tiny portion of the country's people, but by 1770 they made up 21 percent of the population. The chart shows that over the period as a whole the black population grew proportionately faster than the white.

2. Some of the reasons explaining white population growth include large family size, relatively healthy living conditions, ample diet, and, not the least, continuing migration from Europe. Black population increase resulted from the gradual formation of black families and the escalation of the slave trade (which, in turn, was triggered by the declining supply of indentured servants in the late seventeenth century and the continuing need for labor in the colonies).

3. The chart illustrates the peopling of the new world and the increasing opportunity for the emergence of an American culture as more settlers of each race put down roots. The chart also makes clear the colonies' increasing reliance on slavery and highlights the important role slaves played in the American economy.

Chapter 4 - Quotation

Jonathan Edwards, "Sinners in the Hand of an Angry God," Enfield, Connecticut, 1741. One of the most famous and powerful sermons during the Great Awakening.

Chapter 6 - Quotation

Abigail Adams, letter to husband John Adams, 1776, as he is preparing to sign the Declaration of Independence. An early feminist reminder that revolutionary "natural" rights in America were for white men only and that women would use familiar arguments in achieving their liberation.

Chapter 7 - Quotation

Anti-Federalist (Patrick Henry) argument against ratification of the Constitution, Virginia, 1788. In a debate with James Madison, Henry states the classic case that the states, not the people, formed the compact creating the new government. The argument would be reiterated until the Civil War settled the issues.

Chapter 8 - Quotation

Two pronouncements from gatherings of Democratic-Republican artisan groups in 1795: the first is a 4th of July festival supporting Tom Paine's defense of French revolutionary principle against British conservatism; the second a toast at a New York Juvenile Republican Society dinner. Both show the democratic attitude of workers, drawn more and more into the politics of the 1790s.

Chapter 9 - Quotation

Thomas Jefferson, Inaugural Address, 1801. Although seeking reconciliation with the Federalists, Jefferson articulates the Republican program of expansion ("with room enough..."), limited government, equality of opportunity, and religious and economic freedom.

Chapter 11 - Quotation

Regulations from a New England boarding house for women workers in the mills, from the 1820s or 1830s. The rules were an attempt to ensure that women workers lived in a respectable manner and had enough sleep to work efficiently. The regulations highlight the regimentation of life in a mill town but also hint at the sense of sisterhood which these boarding house arrangements often fostered.

Chapter 13 - Quotation

Declaration of Sentiments, Women's Rights Convention, Seneca Falls, New York, 1848. Drafted by Elizabeth Cady Stanton, and modeled on the Declaration of Independence, the Seneca Falls Declaration and resolutions signalled the women's rights agenda for the century to follow.

Chapter 13 - Chart: Public Land Sales, 1815-1860

1. The chart illustrates the pattern of public land sales between 1815 and 1860. The decades of the 1830s and the 1850s saw spectacular increases in the sale of public lands, followed by sharp declines. Note the Panic of 1837 and subsequent depression.

2.   Some of the factors that contributed to the patterns
     apparent here include the opening of new territories
     for settlement, legislation that made it easier and
     cheaper for Americans to acquire land, improvements
     in transportation and the growth of markets that
     made settlement attractive, land hunger on the part
     of both free farmers and slaveholders, large scale
     speculation, and easy banking policies.

3.   The chart as a whole suggests the expansion of
     agriculture (and of settlers) into new western lands,
     the displacement of Native Americans, the impact of
     feverish speculation on the economy, and the periods
     of economic expansion in the 1830s and 1850s with the
     sharp contractions that followed.

Chapter 15 - Cartoon

A Know-Nothing (American Party) cartoon stereotyping the new
Irish and German immigrants of the early 1850s as whiskey and
beer-drinking ruffians who steal off with the ballot box
(presumably to a saloon).

Chapter 16 - Quotation

Abraham Lincoln, Second Inaugural Address, 1865. Delivered
less than six weeks before his assassination, the second
inaugural is one of the most eloquent and stirring
presidential addresses in American history.

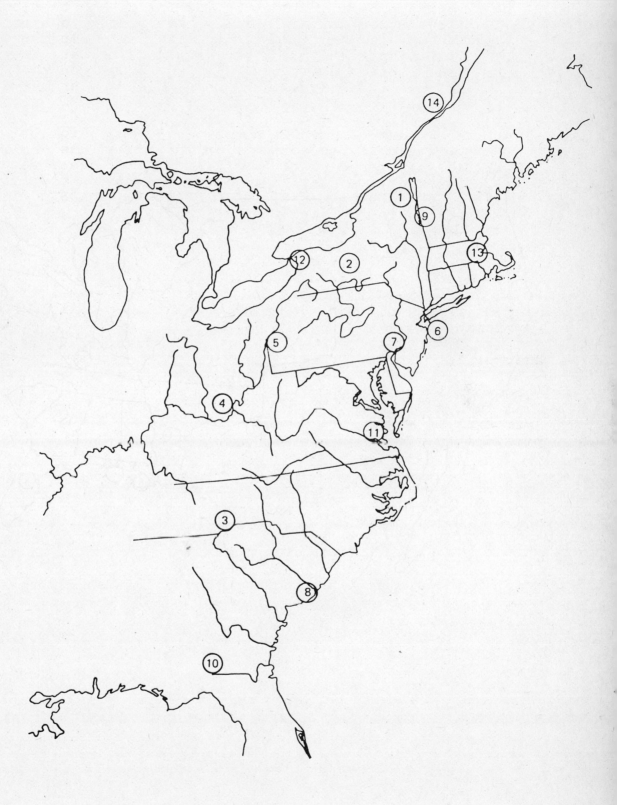

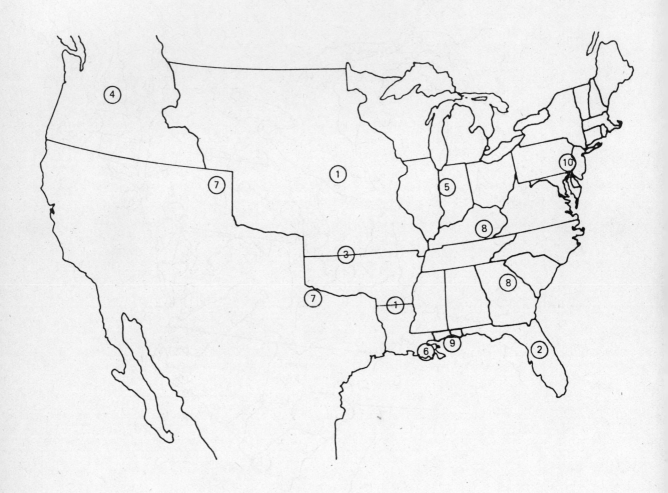

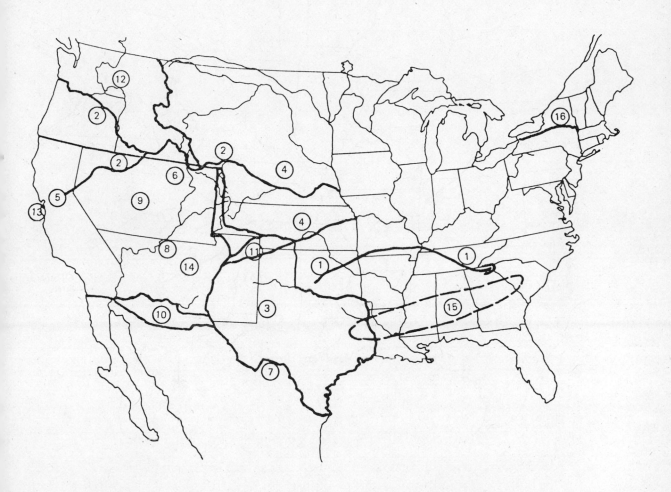

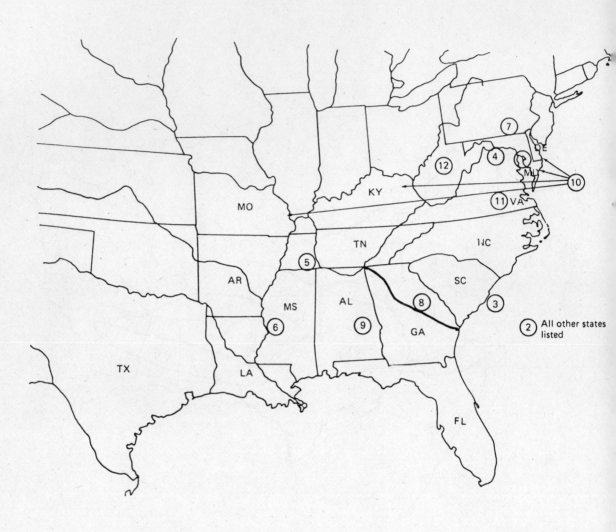